THE SURRENDERED

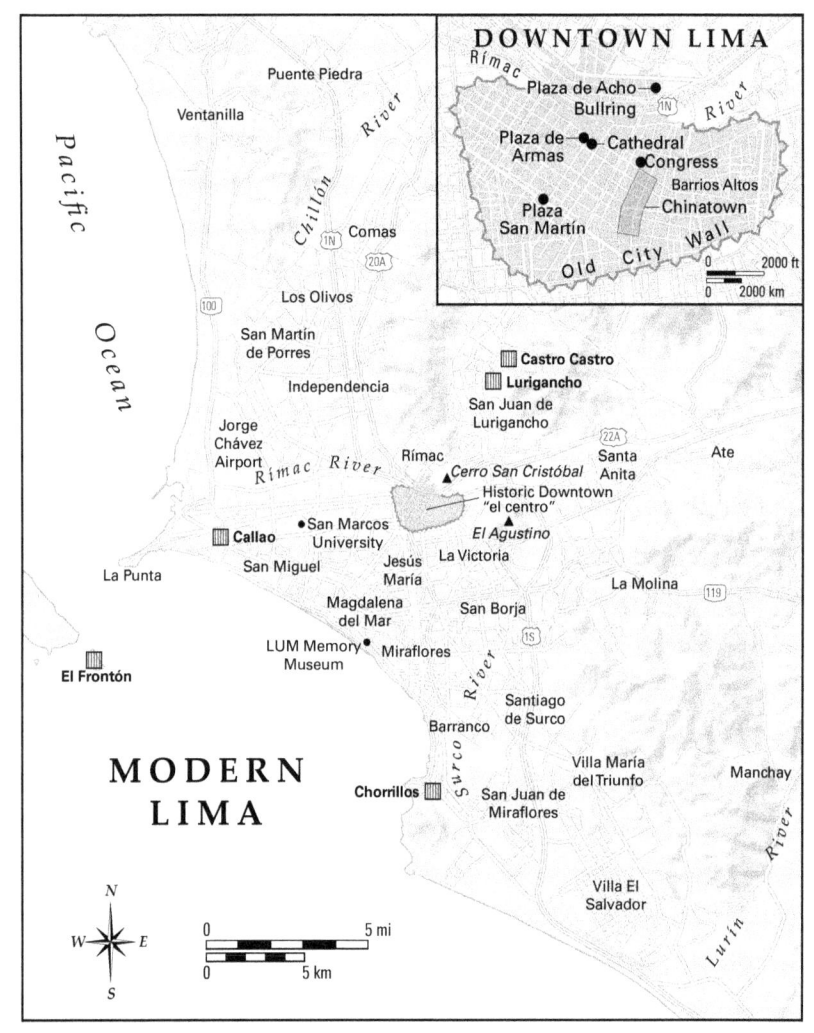

Map drawn by M. Roy Cartography

THE SURRENDERED
REFLECTIONS BY A SON OF SHINING PATH
JOSÉ CARLOS AGÜERO

Translated by Michael J. Lazzara
and Charles F. Walker

Edited by Michael J. Lazzara
and Charles F. Walker

DUKE UNIVERSITY PRESS *Durham and London* 2021

© 2021 DUKE UNIVERSITY PRESS
All rights reserved
Designed by Matthew Tauch
Typeset in Warnock Pro by Copperline Book Services

Library of Congress Cataloging-in-Publication Data
Names: Agüero, José Carlos, author. | Lazzara, Michael J., [date]
editor. | Walker, Charles F., [date] editor.
Title: The surrendered : reflections by a son of Shining Path / José
Carlos Agüero; translated by Michael J. Lazzara and Charles F.
Walker ; edited by Michael J. Lazzara and Charles F. Walker. Other
titles: Rendidos. English
Description: Durham : Duke University Press, 2021. | Includes
bibliographical references and index.
Identifiers: LCCN 2020021177 (print) | LCCN 2020021178 (ebook) |
ISBN 9781478010517 (hardcover) | ISBN 9781478011651 (paperback) |
ISBN 9781478021216 (ebook)
Subjects: LCSH: Agüero, José Carlos. | Sendero Luminoso
(Guerrilla group) | Political violence —Peru—History—20th
century. | Human rights workers—Peru—Biography. | Peru—
Politics and government —1980-
Classification: LCC F3448.7.A38 A313 2021 (print) |
LCC F3448.7.A38 (ebook) | DDC 985.06/3—dc23
LC record available at https://lccn.loc.gov/2020021177
LC ebook record available at https://lccn.loc.gov/2020021178

Cover art: José Carlos Agüero visiting El Frontón. Photo by
Virginia Rojas, 2018. Courtesy of the artist.

In memory of Silvia Solórzano Mendívil
(1945–1992)

and José Manuel Agüero Aguirre
(1948–1986)

*The silence that lives between two words
Is not the same silence that envelops a head as it falls,
Nor that which a tree's presence imprints
When the wind's evening fire fades away.*

*Just as every voice has timbre and pitch,
Every silence has a register and depth.
One man's silence is different from another's,
And not speaking one name isn't the same as not speaking another.*

*An alphabet of silence exists,
But they haven't taught us to spell it out.
Still, the reading of silence is all that lasts,
Perhaps more so than the reader.*

Roberto Juarroz, "El silencio que queda entre dos palabras..."

CONTENTS

Glossary	ix
Timeline	xi
Editors' Introduction	1
MICHAEL J. LAZZARA & CHARLES F. WALKER	
Acknowledgments	19
About These Texts	20
Part I. Stigma	24
Part II. Guilt	41
Part III. Ancestors	58
Part IV. Accomplices	65
Part V. Victims	80
Part VI. The Surrendered	96
A Conversation with José Carlos Agüero	108
MICHAEL J. LAZZARA & CHARLES F. WALKER	
Bibliography	131
Index	137

GLOSSARY

Arguedas, José María (1911–1969) Distinguished Peruvian novelist, poet, and anthropologist. He wrote in both Spanish and Quechua, providing intimate portraits of Andean life and cultural conflict.

ANFASEP Asociación Nacional de Familiares de Secuestrados, Detenidos y Desaparecidos del Perú (National Association of Relatives of the Kidnapped, Detained, and Disappeared of Peru). Founded in 1983, ANFASEP has become an emblematic human rights organization. Its founder and honorary president, Angélica "Mamá Angélica" Mendoza de Escarza (1929–2017), endured threats and gained great prestige and respect for her courage.

DIRCOTE/DINCOTE Dirección Nacional contra el Terrorismo (National Directorate against Terrorism). A branch of the Peruvian National Police in charge of antiterrorism law enforcement, it played an important role in the battle against Shining Path.

Gonzalo (Comrade Gonzalo or Presidente Gonzalo) *See* Guzmán Reynoso, Abimael

Guzmán Reynoso, Abimael (1934–) The founder and absolute leader of Shining Path. A professor of philosophy at Ayacucho's San Cristóbal of Huamanga University, he fostered a cultlike following. He was captured in Lima on September 14, 1992, and is currently serving a life sentence for terrorism and treason.

HIJOS Hijas e Hijos por la Identidad y la Justicia contra el Olvido y el Silencio (Sons and Daughters for Identity and Justice against Oblivion and Silence). An organization of the children of those who disappeared in Argentina under the 1976–1983 military regime.

LUM Lugar de la Memoria, la Tolerancia y la inclusion social (Space for Memory, Tolerance, and Social Inclusion). Peru's Memory Museum, opened in 2015.

Mamá Angélica *See* Mendoza de Escarza, Angélica

Mendoza de Escarza, Angélica (Mamá Angélica) (1929–2017) The founder and honorary president of ANFASEP. On July 12, 1983, her son Arquímedes was taken by the Peruvian military, and he was never seen again. She fought incessantly to find him and others who were detained and disappeared, becoming a national and international symbol of human rights.

MIR Movimiento de Izquierda Revolucionaria (Revolutionary Left Movement). Founded in 1962, it began guerrilla actions in 1965. After the death of its founder, Luis de la Puente Uceda, later that same year, it divided into three factions.

MOVADEF Movimiento por Amnistía y Derechos Fundamentales (Movement for Amnesty and Fundamental Rights). A pro–Shining Path organization that seeks amnesty for Shining Path prisoners.

MRTA Movimiento Revolucionario Túpac Amaru (Tupac Amaru Revolutionary Movement). A more traditional guerrilla group that fought at the same time as Shining Path. The two groups had little respect for one another.

National Coordinator of Human Rights (Coordinadora Nacional de Derechos Humanos) A coalition of Peruvian human rights organizations created in 1985 that remains active today.

NGO Nongovernmental organization.

the P / the Party A nickname for the Peruvian Communist Party–Shining Path

Shining Path The common name for the Peruvian Communist Party–Sendero Luminoso, a subversive group that declared war on the Peruvian state in 1980. According to the TRC, Shining Path committed terrorist acts, was the primary cause of the internal war, perpetrated the most human rights crimes, and had a genocidal character.

terruca/terruco **(terrorist)** Derogatory slang for members of Shining Path or the MRTA and in some cases for anyone who defended them.

TRC Truth and Reconciliation Commission (Comisión de la Verdad y Reconciliación, 2001–2003). Established in 2000 by interim President Valentín Paniagua and President Alejandro Toledo, the TRC presented its findings in a nine-volume *Informe final* (Final report) that is now available at https://www.usip.org/publications/2001/07/truth-commission-peru-01.

Tupamaros A guerrilla movement active in Uruguay in the late 1960s and early 1970s. José Mujica, president of the country (2010–2015), was one of the movement's leaders and spent fifteen years in prison.

Uchuraccay A massacre of eight journalists, a guide, and a local indigenous man in the highlands of Ayacucho on January 26, 1983.

UNI Universidad Nacional de Ingeniería (National Engineering University, Peru).

TIMELINE

1945	Silvia Solórzano Mendívil born in Lima
1948	José Manuel Agüero Aguirre born in Tarma
1967	José Manuel admitted to UNI; never graduates
Late 1960s	Silvia is a member of the Communist Party; José Manuel of Patria Roja (Red Homeland, a Maoist party)
Early 1970s	Parents belong to different subparties within the MIR
1970–1971	Silvia and José Manuel meet, are involved in union work, and spend some time in Huancayo
1972	Birth of José Carlos's sister
1975	Birth of José Carlos
1976	Birth of José Carlos's brother
1977	National strike; José Manuel loses job and is blacklisted
1979–1981	José Manuel is a union leader with Federación de Trabajadores de la Industria Metalúrgica del Perú (Peruvian Industrial Metalworkers Federation)
1980	Launch of Shining Path insurgency
1982	José Manuel and Silvia join Shining Path
1983	Both parents arrested, released in 1984 after about one year for lack of evidence (José Manuel in Lurigancho prison; Silvia in the Chorrillos and Callao prisons)
1985	José Manuel arrested after attack in which a police officer is killed
1986, June 20	José Manuel killed in El Frontón prison uprising
1990	Police come to the family house, make multiple threats
1992, May 26	Silvia is executed by alleged state security agents on Lima beach

1992, September 12 ... Abimael Guzmán, Shining Path leader, is captured

2003 .... TRC releases its final report

2015 .... *Los rendidos* published in Spanish

2018 .... Agüero receives the Premio Nacional de Literatura (National Literary Prize), nonfiction category, for *Persona* (2017)

EDITORS' INTRODUCTION
MICHAEL J. LAZZARA & CHARLES F. WALKER

José Carlos Agüero was a child of Shining Path. Both of his parents fought in this Peruvian guerrilla group and paid with their lives. Frequent changes in residence, clandestine meetings, wounded comrades, furtive exchanges of information or weapons, secrets from his classmates, and the imprisonment and execution of his parents marked his childhood. A historian and anthropologist by training and also a gifted poet, José Carlos has spent much of his life exploring why his mother and father supported this hard-line Maoist party and how we are to understand or approach issues such as violence, guilt, forgiveness, and memory. He bluntly confronts the question of his own responsibility, if any, for Shining Path's acts of terrorism. The search to understand his family and his parents' motivations, as well as violence and its aftermath, lies at the heart of his book.

Los rendidos became an immediate best seller and media sensation when it was released in Peru in 2015. Reviewers lauded it for its fine prose, accessibility, and searing honesty. Many complimented Agüero for his courage and his willingness to share his life as the son of two members of Shining Path at a point when the country was still reeling from the effects of a brutal guerrilla war (1980–2000). According to the TRC's 2003 report, 69,280 people died in the conflict, more than half at the hands of Shining Path.[1] *Los rendidos* was published just three years after another brilliant and highly readable memoir, Lurgio Gavilán Sánchez's *Memorias de un soldado desconocido: Autobiografía y antropología de la violencia* (When rains became floods: A child soldier's story, 2012; 2015 in English). Gavilán's book tells his story as a child soldier in Shining Path.[2] Together, the two books prompted wide-ranging discussions about Shining Path, the role of children in the war, and much more. Among their many contributions, the memoirs punctured the myth that people did not want to talk or read about a very troubling period in Peru's history. To the contrary, public discussion and publications about Shining Path grew exponentially in Peru after the release of these two books, so much so that they became major catalysts for debates on memory and recent history.

Not everyone, however, received Agüero's book with sympathy or enthusiasm. He has frequently been called a terrorist in print and on television. Some conservative commentators have even asked whether his work violates Peru's "apology for terrorism" bans; they have demanded formal inquiries or, worse, have called for his arrest.[3] In May 2018, Congressman Edwin Donayre, a retired general, surreptitiously recorded a visit to LUM, where Agüero had been a consultant. Donayre claimed that his tapes showed that the museum presented a pro–Shining Path viewpoint and that it was brainwashing visitors. Conservatives demanded that the minister of culture, Patricia Balbuena, whose office oversees the museum, testify before Congress. One congressman, Segundo Tapia, asked her to confirm if "the son of two terrorists" (Agüero) was an employee of LUM. Another conservative congressman, Juan Carlos Gonzáles, associated Agüero with MOVADEF.[4] These were notorious examples of a broader smear campaign spearheaded by conservatives, particularly by followers of former president Alberto Fujimori and his daughter, Keiko, to criticize Agüero, belittle his publications (he has other books of nonfiction as well as poetry), and delegitimize his voice. It is but one battlefront in a struggle between human rights activists such as Agüero who seek to debate and learn more about the Shining Path period, the atrocities of the guerrillas, *and* the crimes of the military and those who prefer to declare the 1980–2000 period a closed chapter in Peruvian history and move on.[5]

Agüero has not backed down from these controversies. When we interviewed him in September 2017 for the conversation that appears at this end of this book, he ducked away at lunchtime for a television interview. Without any warning, the TV crew sat him down alongside a woman whose family member had been killed by Shining Path, introducing him not as a historian or author but simply as "the son of terrorists." Agüero handled this sensationalist media trap well, with his characteristic calm and humor. As always, he expressed his opposition to Shining Path's violence, noting that he was sorry about the role the Party played in the conflict; he also stressed that dialogue is the best way to confront such a tumultuous period if Peru is ever to find any kind of solace or perhaps even reconciliation. His book, in short, has left Peruvians divided or has shed light on existing divisions. Thousands of readers have expressed their deep admiration while conservatives continue to cast him as a terrorist (by association) whose work should not be read under any circumstances. Supporters of Shining Path, for their part, have also been critical: they dislike Agüero's critique of the Party as well as his refusal to cast his parents as martyrs or revolutionary heroes, as many other children of Shining Path militants have done. One Shining Path author, Miguel Qorawa, for example, called *Los rendidos* part of a mission to "confirm the official story of the internal war ... to corroborate the state's version."[6] The book, however, does just the opposite. Given the conflicting perspectives and controversies that surround Agüero, it's abundantly clear that what happened during the war and how those events should be remembered and interpreted are still hot-button issues in Peru.

Shining Path emerged in the 1970s out of the multiple divisions that existed within the Peruvian Left. Comprised of Maoists who defended China's Cultural Revolution, the group began its insurgency in 1980, at the very point when democracy was returning to Peru following twelve years of military rule under two radically different presidents: General Juan Velasco Alvarado and his "progressive" military dictatorship (1968–1975), which had advocated for agrarian reform and nationalized key industries, and the conservative Francisco Morales Bermúdez (1975–1980). Shining Path had no interest in reform. Based in the Andean region of Ayacucho, the group detonated change that was radical and fast and that sought to dismantle the entire Peruvian state to liberate the oppressed. To wage the "people's war," Shining Path treated brutally anyone who did not support its cause and attacked areas where the Peruvian state was weak. In fact, it even targeted union leaders, community organizers, and members of other leftist political parties whom it considered far less radical and more conciliatory toward the state.[7] In contrast to other Latin American guerrilla groups, Shining Path militants did not wear uniforms or respect civilians, and they rejected the Geneva Convention's terms of war and the very concept of human rights.[8] The Peruvian state paid little attention to them in the initial years, unconcerned about what was happening in the distant Andean communities in which they operated. But by late 1982, President Fernando Belaúnde (1963–1968, 1980–1985) recognized the danger Shining Path represented and sent in the military, declaring a state of emergency in seven provinces and suspending civil liberties. Frustrated by the mobility of Shining Path, which took full advantage of the mountainous Andes to wage its battles, the military unleashed a brutal campaign against anyone suspected of supporting the guerrillas. Hands were bloody on all sides.

Indigenous peasants found themselves caught between Shining Path and the military and began to migrate massively to Lima and other cities. Throughout the 1980s, Shining Path expanded, and as it did the body count increased. All the while, the Party developed a cultlike following for its leader, Abimael Guzmán, alias "Presidente Gonzalo," a professor from the University of Ayacucho who ultimately became a mythical figure. Guzmán managed to radicalize his followers using intense Maoist rhetoric aimed at overthrowing the state and preying on people's desire to undo centuries of inequality, racism, and discriminatory practices. Intelligence services ultimately understood that capturing Guzmán was the key to defeating Shining Path. After several near misses, on September 12, 1992, they cornered him and some of his inner circle in an ordinary house in an upper-middle-class Lima neighborhood. Shining Path continued the fight, but the loss of its leader and founder ultimately spelled defeat.

President Alberto Fujimori (1990–2000) ruled Peru at the time of Guzmán's capture and took full credit for it—an interpretation that many in the intelligence services reject. Elected in 1990, Fujimori became increasingly authoritarian, shutting down Congress in 1992. In 2000, he resigned after videos surfaced showing his right-hand man, Vladimiro Montesinos, handing out large bribes to members of Congress and others. Fujimori was arrested in Chile in 2005 and extradited to Peru two years later. In 2009, he was sentenced to twenty-five years in jail for mass human rights abuses but was released in late 2017 due to his "failing health." This proved to be part of a quid pro quo between Peru's president at the time, Pedro Pablo Kuczynski, and Fujimori's son, Kenji, who was a member of Congress and promised to stop his party's push to remove Kuczynski from office in exchange for his father's release. In October 2018, however, the Supreme Court rescinded Fujimori's release, ordering him back to jail.[9] Today, his daughter, Keiko, leads his movement; although she, too, faced charges for money laundering, she was released in November 2019 from pretrial detention. Fujimori's supporters continue to claim that he "saved" Peru from terrorism and economic decline. His critics argue that he was a dictator who ruled over a brutal and corrupt regime. This division between the Fujimoristas and their adversaries strongly marks Peruvian politics today. Keiko has twice lost presidential elections by narrow margins in the second round, in 2011 and 2016. Moreover, the Fujimoristas stand at the forefront of those critical of Agüero, the TRC, LUM, and human rights groups.[10]

Beyond the controversies surrounding Agüero and his memoir, his abilities as a writer and the honesty with which he tells his life story explain the success of *Los rendidos*. He never lapses into melodrama and instead recounts the intensities of his life in an almost matter-of-fact way. He deemphasizes death, destruction, and car bombs—though these realities formed the backdrop of his childhood—and instead foregrounds the memory of his parents and the many challenges that he faced as an *hijo de Senderistas*, the child of Shining Path militants. He tackles head-on the issue of his own responsibility (if any) as a child who, on occasion, participated as an intermediary in his parents' militant activities. Throughout the book, he offers deep, pointed, and personal reflections on memory, impunity, guilt, and forgiveness, subjects that even today are difficult to broach publicly in Peru. All the while, his talents as a writer allow him to move seamlessly among personal memories, political and historical commentary, and philosophical and ethical reflection. The blending of such diverse registers, which bridge the individual and collective while placing Peru into dialogue with other cases of historical violence, makes *Los rendidos* a truly unique book.

Throughout the text, the reader senses Agüero searching for a language to comprehend and convey his own experience as well as the violence of the Shining Path period, one that remains so controversial that Peruvians still cannot agree on what to call it. Most analysts use the term *internal armed conflict*, which conservatives energetically oppose, claiming that it places the guerrillas on an equal moral footing with the military. Conservatives prefer the term *terrorism*; others use *civil war*. At the same time, Agüero takes issue with the language from and about the era, pointing out the limitations of dominant paradigms for thinking about and addressing complex scenarios of violence. For example, he distances himself from human rights discourse, questioning its impersonal, bureaucratic rhetoric and its deployment of overly cautious or even euphemistic language. Taking the entire academic field of memory studies to task with equal critical vehemence, he stated the following about *Los rendidos* in a 2017 interview: "I wanted to move away from the comfort that comes from speaking the language of memory studies. . . . In the end, [such language] tricks us by offering optimistic [ways out of] highly complex questions."[11]

Agüero knows that violent conflicts such as the one Peru lived for twenty years are rarely black and white, but rather full of gray areas, what he calls the "impurities" of war (see section 41). In that vein, he seeks to humanize *all* the victims, underlining that they were much more than statistics or collateral damage. He challenges those who would understand the era as a noble fight against "terrorism," pointing out how such an interpretation only justifies horrendous human rights abuses and oversimplifies what was happening in different locales around the country.[12] In the same breath, he categorically rejects the rigidity or even heartlessness of Shining Path defenders who rationalize tens of thousands of dead in the name of a higher, ultimately defeated, greater good. His rejection of orthodox or Manichean views from *both* the Maoist Left and the Far Right emerges, for example, in the painful recollections he offers in the wake of his mother's death. He describes the scorn he felt not only toward members of the security forces who threatened him, killed his mother, and abandoned her body on a Lima beach but also toward a representative of Shining Path who offered to provide him with the names of his mother's executioners in case he wanted to seek revenge.

But Agüero doesn't want revenge. Instead, he prefers to think about what forgiveness might mean in the face of so much hatred. He knows that his parents (and particularly his father) held important roles in Shining Path and could, in that capacity, be seen as perpetrators; yet he also knows they were victims of the Peruvian state that ordered their deaths. His parents, like him and so many others, are therefore inhabitants of a complex and fraught moral terrain.

Throughout the text, Agüero probes and polemicizes the definition of who is "innocent" and who is not, scrutinizing the distinction between perpetrator and victim. Some readers believe that he is criticizing the human rights community for not assuming the defense of Shining Path. He denies this, stressing instead his interest in illuminating gray areas and silenced topics. The relationship between Shining Path and human rights organizations was certainly adversarial and tense. Shining Path disdained the concept of human rights, casting organizations such as Amnesty International as defenders of the bourgeois order.[13] Members of Shining Path executed civilians, set off car bombs, and relied on other forms of violence; they never used uniforms to distinguish themselves from civilians. Furthermore, they counted on their own cadre of lawyers and ridiculed and even threatened human rights activists. Throughout the conflict, Peruvian human rights organizations such as the Asociación pro Derechos Humanos (Association for Human Rights) and the Coordinadora Nacional de Derechos Humanos (National Coordinator for Human Rights) criticized both the armed forces and Shining Path, underlining their disregard for international norms and bringing to light mass killings and other atrocities. These organizations received threats from both sides.[14]

The Surrendered is not an epic tale but the story of everyday Peruvians who played roles large and small in a brutally painful chapter in their country's history. In *Persona* (Person, 2017), which won Agüero the Peruvian Premio Nacional de Literatura (National Literary Prize) for nonfiction, he clearly rejects epic narratives that would seek to redeem complicated historical actors: "Poor us if we [those with links to Shining Path] need an epic poem [*epopeya*] to contest the violence of those who deny what happened. Is it a matter of swapping civilian heroes for military heroes? . . . Instead, isn't it a matter of overcoming all heroic discourse?"[15] To get beyond heroes and villains, Agüero gives readers an on-the-ground, nuanced view of life in the 1980s and 1990s. His story offers no easy solutions, leaving the reader standing on uncertain ground, far removed from the binary of *us* and *them* that so often fuels discussions of political violence.

Silvia and José Manuel

Much of *The Surrendered* revolves around Agüero's parents, Silvia Solórzano Mendívil (1945–1992) and José Manuel Agüero Aguirre (1948–1986), to whom he dedicates the book. *The Surrendered*, however, does not aim to tell the story of their lives. It gives the reader glimpses of those lives, snippets that remain emblazoned on the memory of a child (now an adult) who lost his parents prematurely. It is therefore a long meditation composed of anecdotes, flashes of memory, philosophical musings, and notes from Agüero's personal diaries kept over many long and painful years. In these pages, a son who has lost his parents struggles to make sense of it all.

Agüero's parents were part of the 1960s generation that sought radical change through leftist politics. His mother began in the "orthodox" Communist Party and then moved around from the Trotskyists to the

José Manuel Agüero Aguirre, Silvia Solórzano Mendívil, and their oldest child. Tinajones, Lambayeque, October 1973. From Agüero Solórzano family photo album. Used by permission of José Carlos Agüero.

MIR, which had in its earlier incarnation fought an unsuccessful guerrilla war in central Peru in the mid-1960s. Agüero recalls his mother's political dedication but also her beautiful voice, wistfully noting that she could have been a singer. He seems puzzled as to how she ultimately landed in Shining Path after passing through multiple parties and movements of a much different ilk. Her free spirit, broad culture, and generosity seemed a mismatch with Shining Path's dogmatism and demand for absolute loyalty. In fact, throughout the text, Agüero notes his mother's disagreements with the Party ("the P," as he sometimes calls it), such as when she organized a jail riot in allegiance with common prisoners in Chorrillos, prompting the ire of Shining Path leaders. At times, he questions whether his mother ever wanted to be in Shining Path at all, calling her, ironically, a "second-rate terrorist." For her disobedience, she was ultimately punished severely by both the brutal prison system and Shining Path.

When things got bad, Silvia Solórzano's family and friends urged her to leave the Party and seek safe haven in exile. She was tempted to follow

José Manuel Agüero Aguirre (*third from left*), comunidad campesina Penachí, La Ramada, Lambayeque, April 1974. From Agüero Solórzano family photo album. Used by permission of José Carlos Agüero.

their advice. Why she never chose to flee, even when she knew she was being watched and hunted, mystifies and bedevils Agüero. He hints that his mother's loyalty to his dead father and to her children, as well as to other comrades whom she felt compelled to support, kept her from leaving; she understood that she was trapped in a sinking ship but believed she had ethical obligations to her comrades if not to the Party itself. There is also a sense of inevitability to Silvia Solórzano's fate. After her release from prison in 1984, security forces kept close tabs on her and her husband. Had she decided to get out of Shining Path, both the Party and those who opposed it would have looked upon her as guilty. She was indeed a marked woman and presumably thought there was no going back.

By the late 1980s and early 1990s, we find Silvia Solórzano running a small store at San Marcos University in Lima, typing theses and selling photocopies, books, and other materials to students. The security forces kept an eye on her and visited the store often. On May 26, 1992, just four months before the capture of Shining Path leader Abimael Guzmán, an event that detonated the guerrilla organization's rapid decline, undercover military officers picked Solórzano up at San Marcos University and took her to a beach south of Lima, shooting her three times. Once she was dead, they pinned a sign on her that read, "This is how traitors die," a clumsy attempt to blame Shining Path for her murder—a story that no one believed. More than an effort to weaken Shining Path, Solórzano's execution was an act of revenge, a message from state security forces that all those who supported the movement would be punished. Agüero portrays his mother with deep love and painful remorse about why she never abandoned Shining Path. He discusses the terrible combination of relief and guilt he felt in the days immediately following her execution. He thanks her profoundly for many things, including making sure that he and his siblings did not join Shining Path.

Like Solórzano, José Carlos Agüero's father, José Agüero Aguirre, joined various leftist organizations. In the early 1970s, he met Silvia while doing political work in the Huancayo area, located in the Andes east of Lima. He abandoned his studies at UNI to become a union leader in Lima in the late 1970s. He was imprisoned in July 1977 for participating in and instigating a mass national strike against the Morales Bermúdez military regime.

At that point, the family's economic situation worsened suddenly and drastically: Agüero Aguirre was blacklisted from jobs because people knew he was a union organizer. José Carlos suspects that his father joined Shining Path around 1982, when the Maoist movement was making inroads into Peru's embattled unions. In 1983, Agüero Aguirre was imprisoned again, this time for his affiliation with Shining Path, but was released due to lack of evidence. Soon thereafter he went underground, and José Carlos saw less of him. His father would appear only occasionally at the family home.

The definitive episode came in 1984 when Agüero Aguirre and four comrades attacked a police station to steal arms but were rebuffed. José Carlos's father fled but was captured. At least one policeman died in the altercation, an event that torments José Carlos, who recognizes that his father presumably was responsible for killing at least one person and was therefore the "perpetrator" of a crime. From there Agüero Aguirre was taken to the prison island known as El Frontón, the site of the infamous 1986 massacre in which he lost his life. José Carlos remembers that during his last visit to see his father at El Frontón, Agüero Aguirre warned

Horizonte Obrero (INRESA Workers Union newsletter), July 26, 1977. José Manuel Agüero Aguirre, José Carlos's father, is listed in the fifth line of the second column as one of the union leaders unjustly fired by the company for organizing a strike. Personal copy owned by Charles F. Walker.

his son that he could sense something was amiss and that the family should remain vigilant. He was right.

On June 19, 1986, Shining Path members rioted in three Lima prisons—Lurigancho, San Juan Bautista (El Frontón), and Santa Bárbara—just as the Socialist International was meeting in Lima, at the invitation of Peru's young and dashing president, Alan García (1985–1990, 2006–2011). Hoping to gain worldwide attention and discredit García, the rioters took prison guards and a few journalists hostage and demanded better conditions and freedom for five hundred prisoners. Negotiations led nowhere, and government forces attacked. Shining Path controlled El Frontón, but the navy used grenades and automatic weapons to stop the resistance. Hundreds were killed during the uprising, hundreds more executed in the following days. Agüero Aguirre was part of one of the final groups to surrender. According to one account, a Shining Path prisoner fingered Agüero Aguirre as a leader of the uprising. The navy officers took him aside, tortured him, and then executed him.[16]

José Carlos Agüero had a more difficult relationship with his father than with his mother. He remembers the good times and the bad with mixed emotions. He recalls with great affection, for example, their chess games and how his father taught him the basics of soccer, an important survival skill for getting by in public school. He lovingly recalls his large, dark-skinned father (whom many called El Negro Agüero) dashing off on his motorcycle or failing miserably when trying to start a business to alleviate the family's constant economic woes. He mentions, with pride, that his father would talk to him about politics and answer his questions about the political pamphlets he'd find lying around the house. Because his father was a politicized man through and through, José Carlos has less trouble understanding his father's participation in Shining Path, though he never justifies the actions he took as a member of the Party. The son recalls his father's stubbornness, the fact that he was a man of action, and his father's impatience with many leftists who shied away from their revolutionary ideals and called for participation in elections. All of these characteristics cohere with the image of the resolute, unwavering Shining Path guerrilla.

The Surrendered describes a family hard-pressed for money, always anxious about the threat of arrest, and balancing numerous commitments, both familial and political. Agüero's parents had to steal time away from the Party to spend it with him and his two siblings. When they did, Shining Path members looked askance at his mother for giving attention to her children instead of to the cause. The family, always under threat of being discovered, had to change residences often, which was devastating for young José Carlos and his siblings. While his parents were in jail, José Carlos had to deal with the stigma of being labeled at school as the son of terrorists. He faced ridicule and disdain not only from his friends and the school director but also from extended family members who wanted to distance themselves from their "terrorist" relatives.

But the many pressures of the guerrilla war were not the only challenges on the domestic front. Agüero's mother confronted his father about a lover he had taken, and his father tearfully moved out. José Carlos and his siblings later met "the other woman" while visiting their father at El Frontón prison. His father's mistress was ultimately arrested and dealt a long jail sentence for her participation in Shining Path. Agüero suspects that she may have joined Shining Path at his father's urging.

The experience of the Agüero-Solórzano family reveals that only two possibilities existed within the world of Shining Path: you were either with the Party or against it. The absolute commitment of belonging to Shining Path—a loyalty that, according to Party codes, was supposed to supersede "petty bourgeois sentimentalism" and all domestic bonds—marked the family indelibly in every aspect of their lives, from their daily routines to their time for one another. Throughout the book, Agüero makes these enormous tensions seem mundane, painfully ordinary, which reveals something about how a cataclysmic period in Peruvian history was lived by real people on the ground. The domestic melds with the political in passages that show how history reverberates in the lives of spouses, parents, children, comrades, and neighbors, changing those lives forever. Agüero grew up understanding that at any moment his parents could be arrested, imprisoned, and executed. In the end, they were. Those events marked his life and serve as the foundation for his memories.

Agüero the Author

Since the publication of *Los rendidos*, Agüero has continued to work as an activist, scholar, and editor and to flourish as a multifaceted writer. He has developed the critical views expressed here on human rights language and practices, questioning the search for objectivity and safe discourse. He also criticizes academics for their distance from Peru's intense battles over memory and politics. Agüero relentlessly demands that Peru reassess the period of Shining Path violence rather than simply pass over it as a period of national trauma that needs to be overcome. Nonetheless, he is much more than a critic, a gadfly, or a maverick who operates from the margins. To the contrary, he enthusiastically participates in public debates, collaborates with numerous communities, and has become a respected public intellectual. His empathy and willingness to dialogue have appeased some of his critics, although for many on the right, he will always remain a *terrorista* (by inheritance) who does not deserve a public voice.

Agüero works with numerous social organizations and movements, including those that aid the victims of Shining Path's violence. As he mentions in our interview with him, numerous children of people killed by Shining Path have approached him for help with their own traumas and with coming to terms with their pasts. Among his many activities, Agüero leads a workshop for "victims" (a term he questions) and oversees a project producing podcasts that feature testimonies from the period of Internal Armed Conflict. In these and other activities, he builds on the call by the late historian Carlos Iván Degregori, his mentor and friend, to "humanize" the conflict, to probe its multiple meanings, and to understand its ghastly consequences on a personal and societal level.

Agüero has published several books of poetry, including *Enemigo* (Enemy, 2016). In the award-winning *Persona*, he uses essays, poems, sketches, collages, maps, and photographs to probe his memories and perceptions of the past and present, developing many of the themes and topics he began to raise in *Los rendidos*. With Pablo Sandoval, he has published an oral biography of the historian Carlos Iván Degregori, *Aprendiendo a vivir se va la vida* (Learning to live, life goes by, 2015). Sandoval and Agüero interviewed their mentor in the final months of his struggle with cancer, producing a remarkable portrait; Agüero also helped edit the fourteen-volume *Obras escogidas de Carlos Iván Degregori* (Selected works of Carlos Iván Degregori, 2011–2016). With the distinguished historian Ponciano del Pino, he has published *Cada uno un lugar de memoria: Fundamentos conceptuales del Lugar de Memoria, la tolerancia y la inclusión social* (Everyone is a place of memory: conceptual foundations of the place of memory, tolerance, and social inclusion, 2014), an examination of LUM. He is also the author of the children's book *Cuentos heridos* (Wounded stories, 2017), which—not surprisingly—breaks with tradition and addresses issues of violence and memory, topics rarely seen in children's literature. In addition, he has coedited two anthologies on memory and education.[17] In short, José Carlos Agüero has become an important and inspiring figure who challenges the status quo in a variety of fields, including history, memory studies, poetry, and human rights and activism. All of these strands contribute to *The Surrendered*.

Translating Agüero's book was no easy task. *Los rendidos* is deeply rooted in Peru's social and historical fabric, though it contains many universal themes—guilt, shame, forgiveness—that speak to the experiences of other societies around the world that struggle to mend deep divides after violence and atrocity. Given the complexity of its subject matter, the book does not provide easy answers. Instead, it deploys the rhetorical question as a key feature of its composition and maintains a constant poetic air. Neither essay nor memoir nor testimony nor autobiography nor academic study, Agüero's book contains elements of all of these genres, blending them beautifully into an intimate, self-reflective poetic key. The author intentionally speaks in a fragmented way, fueled by doubt more than certainty. Sixty-seven vignettes, some of which were originally part of a blog that the author maintained, give shape to a book that Agüero says contains no "finished proposals."

Working closely with the textures of Agüero's voice has taught us that the shame that comes from being the son of two people whom Peruvian society calls "terrorists" can manifest even on a linguistic and syntactical level. Throughout *Los rendidos*, we find an *I* who constantly hides and reveals himself in a painful process of self-discovery. In that vein, the book contains an abundant use of the passive voice and of the word *but*, which Agüero deploys to start sentences or introduce questions whose purpose is to tease out additional shades of gray for his readers' consideration. The register of his voice shifts constantly: he speaks at once as a historian, as a human rights activist, as someone who worked for the truth commission, and as a child who played a role in some of Shining

Path's operations. Through it all, the *I* struggles to appear on the page, to know itself, to write an identity.

In one of the book's most moving sections (part II, section 12), Agüero narrates his mother's wake in the family home after her body was found on a Lima beach. To recount this painful scene, he positions himself almost as an external observer rather than as a direct participant. He watches his relatives and their behavior as if he were a fly on the wall. From his removed position, he takes his relatives to task for their false demeanor: they extend condolences and say pleasant things about José Carlos's mother when, he knows, they really thought she was a "terrorist." Throughout the scene, Agüero searches for his mother but never finds her. Her persona eludes him. He cannot articulate who she was, what motivated her, why she abandoned her children for the "cause," or what her final breaths might have been like as she lay dying on the beach. Like his mother at the moment of her death (and in life), Agüero longs for peace. This search is perhaps his book's most salient feature.

The idea of surrender that inspires Agüero's title functions as a leitmotif and acquires various connotations in the text. It alludes to the injustice of his parents' deaths, who died at the hands of state agents in a condition of surrender (but not capitulation). It speaks, as well, to his parents' total commitment, or surrender, to the cause of Shining Path and, conversely, to this group's absolute rejection of ceding ground or accepting the viewpoint of others. Finally, and perhaps most importantly, it speaks to José Carlos's own need to surrender, to make himself vulnerable so that he can ask for and grant forgiveness.

Notes

1. Comisión de la Verdad, *Informe final*. The full report is available only in Spanish, although there is a summary in English. Most analysts now consider 69,280 an underestimate and argue that the death toll actually approached 100,000.

2. For a fascinating dialogue between Agüero and Gavilán, see University of California, Davis, "Shining Path 2016 HIA Agüero Gavilán." For another poignant memoir, see Llamojha Mitma and Heilman, *Now Peru*.

3   Peru has implemented a series of laws that prohibit "apologies for terrorism"—that is, justification or proselytism in favor of Shining Path. See, for example, Article 316 of the Penal Code (2017), legislation enacted by prominent Fujimoristas.

4   Álvarez Rodrich, "Apología."

5   On debates about memory in Peru, see del Pino and Yezer, *Las formas*; González, *Unveiling Secrets*; Milton, *Art from a Fractured Past*; Milton, *Conflicted Memory*; Theidon, *Intimate Enemies*; Uccelli et al., *Atravesar el silencio*; Vich, *Poéticas del duelo*. For a recent overview of Shining Path, see Starn and La Serna, *Shining Path*. Other key analyses include Degregori, *How Difficult*; Gorriti, *Shining Path*; Stern, *Shining and Other Paths*. On rape, see Boesten, *Sexual Violence*.

6   Qorawa, "Prólogo," 11.

7   Degregori, *How Difficult*, 169–70; Comisión de la Verdad, *Informe final*, 8:355–358.

8   On Shining Path's dismissal of the Geneva Convention and, in general, the notion of human rights, see Comisión de la Verdad, *Informe final*, 3:293–318, 8:357.

9   On Fujimori, see Burt, *Political Violence*; Conaghan, *Fujimori's Peru*. On the detention and trials against Fujimori, see Burt, "Guilty as Charged"; Méndez, "Significance"; Ulfe and Ilizarbe, "El indulto." For the global wave of human rights prosecutions, see Sikkink, *Justice Cascade*.

10 For an excellent collection on Peruvian politics after Shining Path, see Soifer and Vergara, *Politics after Violence*.

11 Agüero, "La épica." On the use of the term *terrorist* or *terruco* and stigmatization, see part II, section 4.

12 On the official discourse of Shining Path members as robotic terrorists and the military as heroes, see Milton, *Conflicted Memory*.

13 See, for example, a 1991 Shining Path internal document that asserts, "It has been proven historically that human rights only serve the oppressing and exploiting classes that oversee imperialist and large landowner-bureaucratic states." PCP–Sendero Luminoso. "Sobre las dos colinas," 32. For more quotes, see Comisión de la Verdad, *Informe final*, 3:311.

14 The story of the human rights community in this period is still to be written. A valuable source is Youngers, *Peru's Coordinadora Nacional*. For an overview, see Comisión de la Verdad, *Informe final*, 3:293–318.

15   Agüero, *Persona*, 135.

16   Most analysts believe that President García ordered the executions. In April 2019, García died by suicide just as he was about to be detained on corruption charges. For more on El Frontón, see Aguirre, "Punishment and Extermination"; Rénique, *La voluntad encarcelada*; Feinstein, "Competing Visions"; Ames et al., *Informe al Congreso*; Congreso de la República, *La barbarie*.

17   Uccelli et al., *Atravesar el silencio*; Uccelli et al., *Secretos a voces*.

ACKNOWLEDGMENTS
MICHAEL J. LAZZARA & CHARLES F. WALKER

We thank Ludwig Uber and Odín del Pozo of the Instituto de Estudios Peruanos for facilitating the translation into English. Eliza Davidovna Laura Klotchkova ably transcribed our two-day conversation with José Carlos. Molly Roy of M. Roy Cartography created the map of Lima. We turned to many people for help, but we particularly want to acknowledge the advice of Renzo Aroni, Ruth Borja Santa Cruz, and Marian Schlotterbeck. Carlos Aguirre and José Ragas helped us greatly by tracking down references and offering sound advice. The University of California, Davis, and the MacArthur Foundation Endowed Chair in International Human Rights provided research support. At Duke University Press, we counted on the guidance of the remarkable Gisela Fosado as well as Alejandra Mejía, Ellen Goldlust, Anne Coulling, and two excellent external readers. We also want to mention the encouragement we received from our families. Thank you, Julia, Ana, James and Zoila, María, Sammy.

Above all, we thank José Carlos for his patience and *buen humor* with our inquisitive questions and frequent requests for clarification. We hope this work demonstrates our profound esteem for him as a writer and above all as a person.

ABOUT THESE TEXTS

The nature of this document is somewhat undefined. In formal terms, it weaves together short texts that are both reflections and biographical notes about a violent era. Let's call them simple, nonfictional texts so as not to complicate the muddled field of memory all the more.

Yet the content of these texts isn't arbitrary. They deal with different aspects of my condition: I am the son of two parents who were militants in the Peruvian Communist Party, known as Shining Path, and who died in that difficult situation, murdered extrajudicially.

I've been writing these texts for a long time—for years, really. I shared some of the stories in a personal blog, the kind that gives a false impression that your life exists for someone else who might read what you've written. In my blog, I published the texts I thought were the least pathetic or that I hoped would raise the fewest questions—a useless precaution to take with a bunch of texts that, to be honest, went unnoticed.

I kept the majority of my writings in a folder on my computer without knowing that I'd ever share them, or how I'd share them. At a certain point, I thought about synthesizing them, giving them another form, and rewriting them with academic rigor. But I abandoned that idea. I'll leave it to more talented people to do that. I didn't feel comfortable with it, and I admit that I'm also incapable of it. But I did want to share, in familiar, personal language, some things that matter to me and that might serve a purpose or help someone else.

Because of how I've written these texts, the reader will sense repetition, contradictions, and half-formed ideas. But that's the real style of this book. There are no finished proposals here, only reflections that have changed over time and probably haven't gotten clearer.

I've written this book from a place of doubt, and it's to doubt that it appeals. It doesn't seek to debunk dominant truths about the internal war or the ideas people have about "terrorists" by proposing some different though equally monolithic perspective. Nor does it wish to give a partisan view or justify violence by appealing to the complexity of certain actors' experience so as to relativize their guilt.

Yet people do not write in vain, even when they don't write clearly. I think there are experiences worth sharing—not to save those who lived through them from condemnation, but rather because sharing those experiences might have a positive moral and political impact. Sharing them can help make visible things people would rather brush aside. It can destabilize the unconscious pacts that shape our reality, our history of the war, and its meaning in the present.

It might be worth it to take another look at the guilty, the traitors, the criminals, and the terrorists and, by contrast, at the heroes, the activists, and the innocent—and even at those who are nothing, the spectators, those who view themselves as passive bystanders in this drama. It might be worth it to think about the language we use to talk about certain things. Might doing that affect our perceptions and memories and how we construct them? I'm not sure.

What I do know is that I'm writing this because it's useful to air certain topics publicly, outside the intimacy of people's homes. I think it can help others who've lived through similar situations to mine: the children of terrorists, those who've been militants in subversive organizations, or survivors. There are many people who'd like to speak out but don't have the chance, people in less favorable situations than I.

I don't pretend to represent anyone. When I write, I do it with only one rule: to be honest. I write as if I were writing for myself. And because I'm not unique, I hope there will be other people who see themselves reflected in these pages.

Many of these ideas, reflections, and intuitions—I'm sure the most interesting ones—aren't mine. They've been woven together over time through conversations with close friends. I don't know if it does those friends any good to name them. Still, I'll mention a few, with their permission.

Thanks to Tamia Portugal, who accompanied this process with wit and sensitivity and, in many moments, lent invaluable support; I cannot thank her with enough respect and affection. Thank you, as well, to my colleagues in the Memory Group, especially to my comrade Ponciano del Pino, who constantly inspires new ways of thinking about the topics to which we're both committed.[1] I'm grateful to my dear friends in the Memory Studies Workshop: they've supported and joined me in thinking about uncomfortable themes.[2] Thank you, too, to Marcus Lenzen, who, back when we were notably younger, encouraged me to write down some of my first stories. Thank you to Francesca Uccelli, for reminding me lately that exchanges of ideas are worth pursuing and that close relationships, mutual learning, and affection can weather any distance. Thank you to Goya Wilson, who in a key moment of doubt came to our aid, and to Martha Dietrich, who during several winters listened patiently, carefully, and intelligently to oral versions of these stories. A very special thank you goes, as well, to Rubén Merino, who graced the original Spanish version of this book with an afterword.

Thank you to my siblings for their patience and understanding. They, too, are part of this universe. They feel uncomfortable with an unrelenting past that, thanks to my doing, now returns and reaches outward to touch others.

And thank you to my parents. I don't vindicate them in this book but rather remember them to help others, almost as if they were useful instruments for broaching certain questions and errors. With my feeble wisdom and dispossession of the truth, I'm hopeful that modesty and doubt can invite us to abandon our trenches and feel curiosity about the suffering of people who are different from us or even those we hate. Though they may be different, perhaps they aren't so far removed from us: maybe a reflection of ourselves and an entire generation abides within those we call *our enemies*.

....

1. The Memory Group (Grupo Memoria) was a space for academic exchange that, with the support of the Instituto de Estudios Peruanos (Institute for Peruvian Studies), organized more than fifty sessions from 2011 to 2013 to debate texts within the field of memory studies and on the period of political violence. Founded by Carlos Iván Degregori shortly before his death, the Memory Group was supported by José Carlos Agüero, Ricardo Caro, Ponciano del Pino, Carolina Garay, Sebastián Muñoz-Nájar, Tamia Portugal, Iván Ramírez, Vera Lucía Ríos, Gabriel Salazar, María Eugenia Ulfe, and Rosa Vera.

2. The Memory Studies Workshop (Taller de Estudios de Memoria) brought together young researchers from the Universidad Nacional Mayor de San Marcos (San Marcos National University) and from 2007 onward held both academic and nonacademic activities to debate the period of political violence, primarily with students. Its members were Renzo Aroni, Keyla Barrero, Iván Ramírez, Erik Ramos, María Rodríguez, Gabriel Salazar, Madeline Torres, Katherine Valenzuela, and Natalia Yáñez.

In most cases, the scenes I narrate stem from direct experience. They deal with my family or with how I experienced (and still experience) situations the war thrust upon us. The protagonists of other situations told me their stories directly. I don't pretend to reconstruct my past faithfully because, in part, my memories are shared; in some cases, my siblings tell different versions or variations of our experiences. Above all, facts are a starting point for sharing meanings and arguments, for reflecting on something quite elusive: the subjectivity of public life. I've changed names and places of the events I reveal so as not to implicate anyone I haven't consulted in advance.

1. Stigma

> Does the stigmatized individual assume his difference is known about already or is evident on the spot, or does he assume it is neither known about by those present nor immediately perceivable by them? In the first case one deals with the plight of the *discredited*, in the second with that of the *discreditable*.
>
> **Erving Goffman**, *Stigma: Notes on the Management of Spoiled Identity*

1   You learn to live with shame. To have a family that part of society views as blighted by crimes, a family of *terrorists*, is a concrete reality, like a chair, a table, or a poem.

You internalize shame gradually over time and live it in many different ways. When you're a child, things are simpler but more hurtful: your defenses are still fragile, and you're an easy target. Where are your parents? What do they do for a living? These aren't easy questions to answer. People don't ask them maliciously, but they make you uncomfortable. They're disarming. They hurt, in a way.

You look back, and you think: things weren't so bad. Shame could rarely be seen: you don't have memories of blushed faces, sweaty palms, or mockery. But there's a feeling of inferiority that darkens your days. You can't tell the truth. And not being able to tell the truth strips you of your honor. As a child, you don't understand things in these terms, but you can feel them.

"My parents are in prison, my parents have been detained, my parents are in hiding, my parents are dead." I couldn't give explanations like these, even though they might have brought me some relief—so that on occasion I could stop hiding or faking normalcy to fit in.

Things get better as the years go by. You learn to handle situations. You invent stories that have some degree of truth but also a fair dose of fiction. On rare occasions, you decide to confide in people who seem capable of understanding. You learn to feel out situations to determine if those asking you questions will treat you harshly, coldly, or indifferently.

Shame isn't a feeling: it's something real, a reasonable reaction, though it's not something you can avoid. It's not momentary humiliation. It's not like tripping on a stage in front of a packed auditorium. I'm talking instead about a kind of shame that doesn't need a trigger, that's part of everything you do and of how you relate to others. It builds up for years—with every lie, every silence, every secret, every evasive answer, every story, in long, lonely moments.

How many people did my parents kill? That's not something I need to know. That I can simply pose that question at any moment—and that the question is valid—is what sustains this kind of shame.

2 But there's something else that sustains this kind of shame. I realized it not long ago when I went to a meeting that happened in a tiny room in downtown Lima, a meeting organized by young leftists, anarchists, and university students.

A group of young people gathered to watch a film about a former Shining Path militant.[1] They'd screened similar films in the past. In general, they looked for independent films that could show different viewpoints

---

1. Little by little, we're seeing more films like this appear: *Aquí vamos a morir todos* (We're all going to die here, 2012), by Andrés Mego; *Sybila* (2012), by Teresa Arredondo; *Las huellas del Sendero* (Shining Path's tracks, 2013), by Luis Cíntora; *Tempestad en los Andes* (Tempest in the Andes, 2014), by Mikael Wiström; and *Caminantes de la memoria* (Memory walkers, 2014), by Heeder Soto and Zoila Mendoza. It's curious that films have opened space for certain questions and taboo topics to find public expression.

on the Peruvian conflict, alternatives to those of the NGOs or the perspectives on TV.²

When the film ended, all who were gathered there talked, debated, and enjoyed refreshments in a welcoming, inclusive environment. Everyone agreed it was important for the "other voices" and the "other version" of the war to be aired publicly—even if this could happen only gradually and in marginal spaces (such as at this precarious meeting in a rundown, old house in downtown Lima). The people gathered were not young extremists but rather a laid-back group of kids: critics of Peruvian society, vegetarians, a whole mix. Their comments insisted on a need to dispel myths about the war. Yet, at the same time, they played their part in creating new myths about Shining Path: its freedom-seeking heroism, its egalitarian zeal, its devotion to noble causes, its personal sacrifices for others. They celebrated the guerrillas' altruism and advocated for a need to "recover the context" in which Shining Path acted so that society could better understand the guerrillas' actions—so that people could see that what Shining Path did was political in nature, not just terrorism. In the end, they wanted to humanize Shining Path.

I was surprised at how closely their demands echoed others I'd been hearing recently. Within academia, too, people were pushing to unveil hidden memories and spoke of a need to give Shining Path a human face. Their arguments dovetailed nicely with a critical stance that was starting to emerge in Peru about concepts such as victimhood and innocence." When applied to people affected by violence, these terms tended to erase the complex political processes that give rise to the violence in the first place.

The young people also fiercely critiqued NGOs. They considered them hypocritical for making choices about who would be considered a victim—for categorizing certain victims as defensible and others as inde-

---

2. In Peru, Alberto Fujimori's authoritarian government propaganda rather successfully managed to make the term *NGO* synonymous with terrorist organizations and with those seeking profit from poverty at the expense of society's most vulnerable groups. To create a discourse on political violence, NGOs have used a human rights framework and deployed categories such as *perpetrator*, *victim*, *guilt*, and *innocence*. As in other countries, NGOs in Peru have maintained their own version of the theory of two demons or of the people caught in the crossfire, which has afforded them an identity while allowing them to fulfill their mandate in openly hostile environments.

fensible. Doing this, they thought, turned NGOs into accomplices with the prevailing power structures.

I asked the kids if they thought that we should, in fact, celebrate the brand of unbridled altruism that the Shining Path militant in the film displayed, or if instead we should interpret the pride the young woman took in separating from her family and those in her immediate circle, all in the interest of the revolution, as deeply egotistical. I asked them if giving a "context" to Shining Path was simply a political strategy masked as an intellectual argument seeking to validate certain decisions that had caused great harm.

For quite a while, those present took turns responding to me, their tone growing ever harsher. They felt I was ambushing them. They called me a neoliberal, a petty bourgeois, an academic. But what made me feel even more uncomfortable was that they felt cornered. They felt I was subtly accusing them of being members of MOVADEF.[3] They thought I was treating them like countless others had done every time they dared to give voice to those "other memories." They thought I was launching veiled threats, that I was implying that in that humble house in downtown Lima people were defending terrorism.

I listened quietly. I wouldn't have wanted to come across as overbearing. I asked myself seriously if I had been—if there was any way to ask these questions without an implicit tone of condemnation or judgment.

Then I remembered a similar experience from my past, which made me choose not to respond in the moment. I wanted to avoid the inevitable betrayal of language: its inability to speak without implicating the speaker. When one touts an air of moral superiority, it becomes hard to listen to others who have something different to say. Either they are obliged to keep silent, or they default to a politically correct way of speaking to stave off any suspicion that they're terrorists.[4]

---

3. MOVADEF is an arm of the Peruvian Communist Party–Shining Path that today is legal and wants to participate in elections but refuses to renounce the ideology that fueled its war. One of its main agenda items is amnesty for its jailed leaders.

4. I remember having done exactly this when I invited two friends to present to the Memory Studies Workshop in 2012. We were talking about new ways to research and approach the experience of Shining Path, particularly in prisons. The use of expressions such as *political prisoner* to talk about members of Shining Path or the MRTA made me feel as if it were my responsibility, given that I was the one organizing the sessions for

As the meeting drew to a close, an energetic young woman, who must have been around thirty years old, looked me straight in the eye and announced clearly and forcefully that she was not at all ashamed of her parents. "That's what you implied, right? Well, not me! I'm proud of what my parents did in the war because they did it for the good of others," she contended. Quiet muttering throughout the room validated her stance. Soon the meeting ended, we shook hands, and I left.

The shame that stemmed from this experience isn't the kind that manifests through feelings. It's not the shame of a blushed face or sweaty palms. It's a way of being that implies rejecting pride, refusing to create myths, and being willing to give up the safety that comes from having a pristine family legacy. It requires embracing a fragile kind of speech that doesn't shy away from the word *perhaps*. It requires acceptance—systematic acceptance—free of alibis.

And what do you have to accept? You have to accept that members of your family, your dearest friends, or people in your inner circle committed acts that resulted in deaths, that those acts weren't just errors. You have to accept that they did these things of their own free will—and not simply because the rebellious generation of which they were part compelled them to act in certain ways.

You have to accept that they understood that their decisions would lead to collateral damage (within their families, in their neighborhoods, among their neighbors, and among the innocent, who do indeed exist). As often happens in wartime scenarios, they saw this collateral damage as an acceptable cost that they weighed against a greater good. You have to accept that war is not the same as peace, even though injustices and social conflicts never go away.

The Peruvian war was brutal and atrocious. Still, it can't be compared to the postwar period, although it's true that certain constants make it tempting to erase the differences between past and present (such as poverty, exploitation, and racism).

....

an auditorium full of undergraduates, to point out that no terminology is innocent, that all terms have a genealogy, and that, consequently, using certain terminology without explanation could lead students to assume that there was academic consensus about it. I merely made everyone uncomfortable and caused one of my invitees to feel obliged to "publicly put a stop" to any apologies for terrorism. So, unintentionally, I became part of the machinery of censorship, and I isolated my colleagues even more.

You have to accept that fathers, siblings, cousins—even you—bear responsibility in a long chain of reasoned and willfully made decisions. To accept these things is to give up self-protection.

If people are unwilling or unable to let down their guard, then they will never feel shame at all. But I'm not convinced that this is necessarily a bad thing. Believing that shame isn't worthwhile serves as a balm to many. Why not let everyone deal with their difficult pasts in the best way they know how?

Take the young woman who spoke that night with conviction and clarity, or the others who supported her in that room. Shame doesn't serve her—or them. Instead of letting down their guard, they struggle, as young leftists, to find their place in the world. They question the world itself, faithful to family legacies that make sense to them only when they act and respond in sync with those legacies.

3   One afternoon Gonzalo said to me, "That's it. I've decided. From now on I want people to call me Ricardo." He didn't need to explain further.

I'd known him since we were kids. For quite some time, I'd been vaguely aware that he was arguing with his mother. She would get on his case, saying he wasn't proud of his birth name. After a lot of back and forth and a complicated legal process, a judge granted him permission to change it. I congratulated him, cautiously.

"I don't know if I'll be able to get used to it," he told me. "Just give it time," I replied. He was chewing on chamomile leaves and staring off into the distance. From a neighboring apartment, we could hear the undulating, tropical rhythms of a song by the band Guinda. It had a happy beat, but its lyrics were about suffering and falling out of love.

We stayed quiet for a long time, drinking our tea, sip by sip, paying silent homage to my friend's lost name. With our simple, silent ritual, we celebrated and lamented that name. His parents had come up with the best name they could think to give him back in 1987: the name of their leader, Presidente Gonzalo. We knew of other kids who'd been given similar names, and we'd often laugh about it. Shining Path's enthusiastic young militants parented no small number of Lenins, Maos, and Stalins. We met one kid named Fal, whose name derived from an acronym for the lightweight automatic rifles (*fusil automático ligero*) that Shining Path used to wage its urban guerrilla war. We also met a girl named

Ila, whose name evoked another Shining Path emblem: the beginning of the armed struggle (*inicio de la lucha armada*). Ila is now dead. Lots of kids back then were baptized with names steeped in the promise of revolution.[5]

We said goodbye to one other. Gonzalo walked me out of the neighborhood so I wouldn't get mugged. "It's just that you seem like a yuppie now," he said to me, half in jest, but warmly. When we got to the bus stop, I shook his hand, and we wished each other's families well. Then I watched him walk off toward the neighborhood market.

His name isn't Gonzalo anymore. It no longer evokes that nightmare of a leader. The name that brought him so much suffering no longer marks him. Watching him from that angle, with his back to me, heading off to buy bread "like any other little Peruvian" (to quote a poem by Teresa Cabrera), I couldn't see the invisible mark that lingers in him.[6] But it was there. He didn't look better or worse, nor did he look more complete or incomplete. Only the two of us managed to see beyond the name that used to be there.

Perhaps, though, the fact that he erased his name will, in the end, mark him even more indelibly—not just in his words and his persona, but in his memory, like an infinite stain.

4   When someone reveals something about you, it makes you vulnerable. At some point in time, or at many points, it happens. Secrets are never perfect, especially secrets like ours that so many people knew about—from the police, to members of community organizations, to my parents' Party comrades, who were constantly being detained and tortured.[7] It sounds nice to call it a "public secret"; it makes for a pretty metaphor.

---

5. A friend once told me about a period of time in which many girls were named Nora, a dark homage to Abimael Guzmán's first wife.

6. "Amor o madre aguardo / como cualquier peruanito / su forma de pan en el desayuno / u otra presencia / aún más olorosa y divina." (Love or mother I wait / like any little Peruvian / your form of bread at breakfast / or some other presence / even more fragrant and divine.) Cabrera, "Como cualquier peruanito," in *Sueño de pez o neblina*, 53.

7. The militants I met from the Peruvian Communist Party–Shining Path never called their organization Sendero; they knew that the press had invented that term. They preferred to speak instead of "the Party," or "the P," for short.

But in real life, public secrets are messy, fleeting, tacit pacts of silence. They work like concentric circles: everyone is in the know, but to greater or lesser extents.

When we lived in Lima's El Agustino district, our closest neighbors knew exactly what my parents were up to and what was going on in our house. Other neighbors who lived down the block—or on the next block—knew too, but in less detail. People who lived farther away had their suspicions and reacted to us differently. Some acted in solidarity or showed us little signs of support; others sympathized more discreetly with my parents because they thought my parents were "fighting for social justice." Still others criticized my parents, but always under their breath, because they feared the Party. It's strange to say, but we knew that people were afraid of us, and we used it to our advantage, to protect ourselves.

Around that time, we had a friend named Benito, a member of Shining Path who'd been captured and likely tortured. We feared he might betray us by telling his torturers my parents' names. When we found out Benito died, we had to flee our home.[8] A few days later we returned briefly to gather some of our things. When we got there, some of our close friends told us details about the police raid and certain neighbors' names who'd helped them carry it out.

They pointed out a group of people who told the police we were terrorists. They mentioned others who had given the police information or told them about "suspicious people" frequenting our house. They also mentioned people who defended us: neighbors who weren't at all political but who held my mother in high regard, who considered her a fighter for social justice. They were the ones who kept the police from ransacking our house and stealing our things. We didn't have much, but what we had was important to us.

Those were tough times, so it was hard to get mad at anyone. At the end of the day, we thought our neighbors' reactions were normal and

---

8. Benito was from the provinces, perhaps from Ancash, and often came over to our house when we lived in El Agustino. My family loved him for his kindness, for how tenderly he treated the children, and for his timidity. We had to flee our home because it was quite possible that he'd been tortured before he was killed; in that state, anyone could inform on his comrades or be captured with others connected to him. In either case, the police could have confirmed that our house was supportive of Shining Path.

predictable. After all, they had to protect themselves. At the same time, though, I still remember how deceived I felt by one neighbor in particular. She lived very close to us and had two babies, in dire poverty. My mother often spoke to the woman about the abusive relationship in which the woman was trapped, offering her advice and treating her like a relative who needed shelter. My mother never tried to involve her in politics or in any matters related to "the P," the cryptic way in which Senderistas referred to the Party. We constantly shared with her what little food we had and regularly took care of her babies.

She was the one who betrayed us most hatefully, most scornfully! "That woman is a *terruca*! She's the leader!" the neighbor told the police about my mother.[9] I'm not sure if the whole time we were helping her she really hated us. Perhaps she just wanted to exist. Perhaps this was her opportunity—her one and only chance to exist somewhere other than on the bottommost rung of poverty's ladder. For a brief moment, she imagined a rung even lower than her own: ours! Because in addition to being poor, we were also dirty.[10]

---

9. *Terruco* has become so hegemonic that it now describes not only the terrorists themselves but also the entire period of violence, which is called "the time of terrorism." It takes on greater meaning as part of an authoritarian-military discourse that tried to become Peru's official memory. See, among others, Degregori, *Qué difícil es ser Dios*.

10. I think it's relevant to share one more doubt. When one of my two siblings read this text, he didn't agree with my description of our neighbor's actions. In contrast to my version, my brother remembers her as one of the people who most defended us. The basic outline of the situation remains unchanged: when faced with danger, our neighbors debated whether to accuse us, defend us, or play dumb. I think my memory is accurate, and I know that the most important thing isn't how faithful I am to an isolated fact. But, when I wrote this episode, I was thinking about this particular woman and not another. I wasn't thinking about our neighbor, one of the leaders who worked to make sure every child had milk, nor was I thinking about our cynical neighbor, the one who lived in a wood-planked house . No, I was thinking about this particular woman, who was at the bottom of the heap. This led me to tell the story in a certain way and to share certain reflections. I gave meaning to an event by considering a specific person's attributes, not just her conduct. Yet if it hadn't been she (even though I think it was), would the reflection hold up? I'd have told more or less the same story, but perhaps I'd have come to different conclusions. That's why we shouldn't forget that reflections like those I'm offering in this book are but small contributions to a slow and complex process of debating the violence. These reflections should complement larger research efforts.

5   A neighborhood friend, a boy in my brother's class at school, showed up at our house the day before yesterday with a newspaper clipping. "Is this your mother?" he asked. A full-color image on one of the newspaper's inside pages showed a woman lying on her back, stretched out on the beach. There was a sign on top of her that read, "This is how traitors die." In the note, the woman's first and last name appeared, though slightly altered, probably because of the journalist's failure to copy the police report correctly.

"Yes, it's her," I said.

I waited to see what would happen, how he'd react.

"The good part," I told him, "is that my mother is an anonymous Shining Path militant, not one of the leaders. She isn't one of those women about whom a lot has been written, like Abimael Guzmán's closest female comrades."

My mother's death didn't matter to anybody. It didn't grab major headlines, only brief mentions on morning television and in a few newspapers. She was, in a matter of speaking, a second-class terrorist who they claimed was supposedly killed by her own comrades.[11] She wasn't worth anyone's time. She wasn't newsworthy.

There my friend stood, discovering the secret—waiting. He was a simple, very poor young man, who now works hard running a printing press to support his family. He hugged my brother. And he kept our secret. So did four million television viewers who saw what happened but chose not to see.

---

11. As far as I have been able to tell, agents of the Peruvian Army killed my mother extrajudicially in May 1992. Similar actions took place in both Lima and the provinces throughout the early months of 1992. See, among others, Comisión de la Verdad, *Informe final*; Uceda, *Muerte en el Pentagonito*. The sign found on her body, supposedly authored by Shining Path, gives reason to believe it was forged. After being detained at the exit to San Marcos National University, where she worked typing up students' papers on an old typewriter, she was shot three times and then her body was abandoned on a beach in Lima's Chorrillos District. Various witnesses saw her get into the truck that captured her on University Avenue while she waited for public transportation to take her home.

6   I can only imagine what it's like to be exposed to public scrutiny and scorn. My family belonged to the world of unorganized militancy. They certainly had their share of adventures and misadventures, but they were essentially waging a silent war, a small-scale war, a war happening on the outskirts of Lima in the "cones," in various districts and humble shantytowns full of shacks covered with makeshift roofs.[12] They had few *medios* with which to fight, and the weapons they did have were quite old.[13] They were young, Senderista men and women living in countless homes spread throughout the city that gave them temporary shelter. Their struggles and battles weren't epic.

The police were not much better off. They were equally exposed and left to their fate. They had routines very much like those of the militants: sleuthing, harassing, pursuing people, showing up a moment too late, with only occasional success. Their families lived in the same poor neighborhoods as their enemies, and their weapons were just as precarious.

It was a relentless war—a war without bloody trenches or barbed wire, without newspaper coverage of the mass graves being discovered in the Andean highlands, without reports or spectacles.[14] All were left on their own to count their dead silently.

All of these people belonged to the same generation: young police officers who were really adolescents, practically children; the subversives; and the army recruits, many of them forced into service and who now languish, forgotten, in their towns. All of them killing one another! It was like a war among children, and this made it so much grayer. It makes

---

12. *Conos* (cones) refers to the large districts that formed on the outskirts of Lima when migrants moved from the Andean highlands to the capital in the mid-twentieth century, a process that accelerated because of the forced displacements that the war sparked. The cones were impoverished areas that grew in a disorderly way. Today they are like large cities unto themselves within the new metropolitan Lima.

13. The Shining Path militants I met used the colloquial term *medios* (resources) to refer to their old pistols, revolvers, rifles, and explosives. Taking care of one's medios was almost a sacred thing, given their scarcity and the high human cost of obtaining them.

14. Since at least 1983, both the press and the national and international human rights organizations have presented evidence of massacres, torture, and mass graves (especially what was happening in Andean regions such as Ayacucho, Apurímac, and Huancavelica) in chronicles, reports, accusations, and photographic exposés.

me think of something from a character in *All Quiet on the Western Front*: We showed up dreaming of our futures, believing in what our teachers instilled in us, believing in what adults said, but the first death, the first decimated body we saw, put an end to that order.[15]

My parents and their friends were just common Senderistas. Others weren't so lucky: they were high-profile figures, had noteworthy captures, were foreigners, or held important positions. Because of their notoriety, they've lived exposed for years, either in jail or stalked by the news media. Once they were released from jail, many of them found it hard to create spaces in which to piece their lives back together. Do they miss prison? There, at least, they had friends.[16] In the outside world, they're surrounded by the hatred and fear of those who label them infectious agents. Do they deserve such treatment? Yet how can they not warrant suspicion, mistrust, or even resentment and hate if families today mourn their dead because of the things these people did?

But is it enough to say that Shining Path's militants deserved what they had coming, that they should simply accept the consequences of their actions indefinitely without ever being afforded any consideration? Does forgiveness have a "time," just as memory, as academics say, has a time?[17] What fate would those who belonged to Shining Path have to suffer to make us feel at ease or more satisfied? Would they have to be exiled, disappeared, ostracized, forgotten, or left destitute? Is that all we can offer them?

7 Some films have been circulating, on a small scale, among people interested in the topic of memory: a handful of biographical films and

---

15. Remarque, *All Quiet*, 291.

16. Martha-Cecilia Dietrich's 2015 documentary, *Entre memorias* (Between memories), delves into this subject: MRTA women, some in prison and some not, who are taking stock of their lives.

17. *Temporalities of memory* is a phrase that memory scholars commonly use to refer to several things: that it's easier to remember a painful and complex occurrence the more time has passed since it happened; that the opportunities to hear new voices and points of view about the past shift in accordance with people's willingness to remember the past, forget it, or reinterpret it; and that there's no single road to forgetting or remembering. See Degregori, "Sobre la Comisión"; for a much more detailed and historicized treatment of these topics, see Stern and Winn, "El tortuoso camino."

lots of films about prisons, especially about the experiences of female prisoners. It's striking to see such a growing interest in topics that were once considered taboo and somewhat risky.

But what might the people represented in these films think about how they're portrayed? What might they say about how artists are interpreting them?

It must be hard for the Shining Path militants portrayed in these films to rest. They can't really protest or demand greater respect. What rights can people protest when they have lost all rights?

Many years have passed, and Shining Path militants continue to be a pretext for banal performances of feigned understanding. We all can talk about Shining Path because doing so makes us look better. We shine next to them. We appear more magnanimous. And when we face them protected by our ethics, our reason, and our impeccable democratic spirit, we skirt the real issue and take comfort in our difference from them.[18]

It's so difficult to approach our enemies—or the guilty—with any real willingness to understand them. I'm not saying that we should agree with them or forgive them. Nor should we try to defeat them in an ideological battle. I'm talking about simple understanding—with no compensation and no reward or recognition for being an empathetic hero. It's tough because we don't get anywhere in society by trying to understand our enemies. It doesn't bring us prestige. And if we were to show empathy, no one would notice.

---

18. This is what Arredondo does in her documentary *Sybila*, a personal, almost egotistical coming-to-terms with the myths of her childhood. In the process, she shows no concern for the damage that such exposure might cause the protagonist's family, a family that has had to confront not ghosts but rather years of very complicated experiences. The film undoubtedly has merit because it shows some decisive moments: particularly how an impatient and harshly rational woman from Shining Path constructs her arguments. But it does this through an ambush whose goal is to show how very different the director-narrator is from her protagonist. Articles in the press that celebrated the film also expressed amazement at the director's empathic approach: they said, let's try to understand this exotic woman who draws us close and pushes us away, who at bottom is unknowable to us but seems human. Yet if the exercise were instead to switch roles, would it be so simple to write this way, claiming authority to grant understanding or even humanity? I think that to understand the other is, in a way, to die with the other, to give oneself over to another person. But it's not always possible to do that, nor is it even right to ask someone to do it.

To treat the families of "innocent" victims with empathy is a different story. In that case, we gain something almost immediately. That's why there are so many activists, artists, memory promotors, and cultural mediators. Wasn't it Todorov who, suspicious, warned us that those who lead the fight for memory and morality might be doing it to feel better about themselves and to secure their status as exemplary individuals?[19]

When someone acknowledges the "legitimate" victims, it really doesn't matter if the approach is childish, mechanical, or disingenuous. People celebrate the mere gesture as intrinsically just, as ringed by a halo of goodness. There are extreme cases (which perhaps aren't so rare), such as that of an urban artist who travels all over the place with a stencil of the likeness of Mamá Angélica, the great Peruvian human rights activist. Within five minutes, that artist can multiply Mamá Angélica's image wherever he feels it's missing. Another example comes to mind of a different artist whose collages combine images of Ekeko (the god of abundance), Japanese *manga* characters, and other elements of Lima's *chicha* cultural melting pot, as well as the victims' faces and other iconography related to them.

But nothing is simple. Human rights organizations feel affection for these artists. They are grateful to have them as allies, as companions in their quest for justice and reparations—especially when no one else does anything and the state remains so indifferent. Despite the banality of their art, these artists accompany the victims and their families in solidarity. And solidarity is no small thing.

So, it's hard to make clear judgments about anything. Ultimately, the use and abuse of memory is something that has no clear limits but rather, perhaps, only moments and needs.

---

19. "Ritual commemoration, when it only confirms a negative image of the other in the past or a positive image of the self, is ineffective as a tool of public education.... It is often said nowadays that there is no statute of limitations on the rights of memory, and that we should all be fighters on its side. But when we hear such appeals against forgetting and for the 'duty of memory,' we should realize that we are not being asked to undertake any recovery of memory—through the establishment of facts or through their interpretation. Nothing and no one stand in the way of such work in democratic states like those in which we live. What we are being invited to undertake is the defense of a particular selection of facts that allow its protagonists to maintain their status as heroes, victims, or teachers of moral lessons, against any other selection that might give them less gratifying roles." Todorov, *Hope and Memory*, 175.

8 It's inevitable for the victims to be an object of study, opinion, and representation. It's also inevitable for the guilty, the enemies: the subversives, the terrorists, the Senderistas. And it's inevitable for the families and heirs of all these people. Perhaps they'd prefer to forget. But they can't do anything to stop others from exploiting their experience because, even though the experience is theirs and theirs alone, it no longer belongs to them.

I remember Milan Kundera's reflections on compassion: a discredited, blighted word for the Peruvian Left, which instead always preferred to speak of solidarity. Kundera spoke of one sense in which we might understand compassion: as a true, impassioned sharing in another's suffering.[20]

With the best intentions, some academics and artists rescue memory and strive for societal recognition of *all* memories—including those of the men and women of Shining Path, or of the MRTA. But there is no trace of compassion in their approach, nor should we expect it. People react in whichever way suits them best.

Yet I think that to lack compassion is a weakness. People never stop to consider (or let themselves feel) that in the process of trying to get to know another's experience they may really be invading the privacy of families that have already suffered so much and that are tired of being the main characters in local tales of infamy.[21]

9 "Tell that boy to go home," I overheard her say. The words emanated from the kitchen. She spoke them in a deep tone that she tried to keep hushed. I could sense a tiff brewing. My friend, almost certainly

---

20. The story's narrator says: "In languages that form the word 'compassion' not from the root 'suffering' but from the root 'feeling,' the word is used in approximately the same way, but to contend that it designates a bad or inferior sentiment is difficult. The secret strength of its etymology floods the word with another light and gives it a broader meaning: to have compassion (co-feeling) means not only to be able to live with the other's misfortune but also to feel with him any emotion." Kundera, *Unbearable Lightness*, 20.

21. Perhaps it's because language sets traps that make it hard for us to understand one another. Ulfe and Ilizarbe ("Paloma") find themselves perplexed by a woman from Shining Path who was at once "a dove and rigid as steel." In Mikael Wiström's 2014 film,

ashamed, told her mother that she had just invited me over to play Monopoly. How was she now going to tell me that I wasn't allowed in her house? Confusion ensued, muttering, pots clanging. I heard an authoritarian-sounding voice that I couldn't quite decipher. Frozen in the entryway, standing in front of a partially cracked-open door of metal and glass, I couldn't move a muscle. I felt so much rage and confusion. I hadn't done anything to deserve this. It wasn't my idea to go to their house! My friend had invited me! My pride was wounded. My legs stayed still, and there I stood: it was as if I wanted to hear my friend kicking me out so that she would feel guilty and I would feel sad. The perfect drama! But it didn't happen that way. Her older sister stepped outside and, in the most polite tone she could muster, said, "I'm sorry. My sister has to study. She can't play with you." And she closed the door.

Twenty years later in a café in the San Miguel Mall, a young woman told me that she had spoken of me to her family at a gathering of aunts and uncles who knew me—or who knew my family. They told her about all the terror they'd lived through because of us. They told her to stay far away from me because I would only wind up ruining her career. They said I was angry and resentful, that assuredly all I wanted to do was take revenge on everyone because of what happened to my parents. She told me all of this at great length and in great detail. She emphasized that those were her family's opinions but that she thought differently. She just wanted me to tell her the truth, to help her decide whose side to take.

The truth . . . The only truth that occurred to me at that moment was the most obvious one: that her family was concerned about her, that they had reasons for feeling as they did, that in their memories my mother

---

Tempestad en los Andes, one of the protagonists, a young woman, asks herself the same question when she tries to explain the actions of her aunt, the Shining Path leader Augusta La Torre. The woman, Josefin Ekermann, cries and can hardly utter the following words: "I can't understand it because she was so tender and at the same time so harsh" (my paraphrase). Language traps us because it forces us into dichotomies; it forces us to affirm ourselves so strongly that it becomes hard for us to identify with others in simple ways. Who is not harsh and also sweet and sensible? Why can't we start by accepting that we're faced with people who, if they aren't our equals, are very similar to us? Ekermann became a respected human rights defender; she died in the March 2019 Ethiopian Airlines crash outside of Addis Ababa.

was, above all, a plague who put everyone she touched at risk. These people had never seen me before. But their memories of my mother made them view me as an extension of her, as resentment incarnate, a Senderista in my very DNA, to my core, an infectious agent. That's what they believed. And because of their fear and desire to protect a family member whom they loved, they never stopped to think about what someone else might be feeling, what I or my family might have experienced. They never stopped to consider that maybe I wasn't a suicide bomber poised to exact revenge on the world.

Of course, I didn't say all this to her. I just shared the gist of what I was thinking. "Your family loves you," I said. "They're worried about you. I don't feel like talking about this anymore." And that's where we left it.

ii. Guilt

because I nourished you with this reality
half-cooked
with many poor flowers of evil
with this absurd flight skimming the swamp
ego I absolve you of me
labyrinth my son

Blanca Varela, "Casa de cuervos"

10   A guy came into the shop we had at San Marcos University and asked me, "Does Silvia Solórzano work here?"

"Yes," I said.

"I'm here to inform you that she died this morning."

"OK."

We were both very serious. He peered at me uncomfortably from behind his black tortoiseshell glasses. I stared back at him silently, waiting to see if he had anything to add. He made no other gesture, said nothing more. He offered no condolences. He didn't look sad. I didn't show any emotion either.

It was a strange day. My cousin, who had enrolled with me at the university that year, came into the store and told me some funny stories. I think he invited me to his house for lunch or dinner. I told him I couldn't make it, that I had things to do. I didn't tell him what I had just found out. I was accustomed to not talking about such things.

All morning, my uncle and I kept going over what had happened, discussing it with the neighboring shopkeepers. "Yes, it was Señora Silvia. We saw her this morning on the news." Everyone saw her but us, because we didn't have a TV. My uncle went out for a while, hoping to find out more details. I stayed back at the store, thinking about the next steps I'd have to take.

It was overwhelming to think about what would come next. The police would show up at our house. I'd have to prepare the scene and hide anything incriminating. But, thinking it through more carefully, why would I have to hide anything now—books, fliers, documents?

What most overwhelmed me was having to talk to my extended family, having to listen to their laments, their complaints, or both—their fake tears. I stalled as long as I could before I went home.

I took a bus. I sat in the back. Since my glasses were pretty crooked, I took them off to rest my eyes. The bus and everyone in it were a blur. Feeling invisible because I couldn't see anyone, I then experienced the most profound and real sense of relief I'd ever felt. I felt relief wash over my being, as if *rest* were more than just a word.

Finally! Finally, after so many years, my mother had finished dying. I'd never again have to wait up for her until dawn. I'd never have to ask friends or acquaintances about her after she'd been gone for days on end. There'd be no more jails, no more visiting her in prison, no more begging her to flee the country, no more sleeping with one eye open waiting to hear the sound of her footsteps at the door, no more hearing her scold our dog Jaky for barking when she'd come home. No more of any of it.

I must have felt all of this while sitting at the back of that rickety bus, alone in my little corner of the world. And while I was feeling all of this, at the very same time I was wracked with guilt. I wanted to cry to counter the relief I was feeling with some outward expression of pain. But I couldn't. I had things to do. That's how I'd been taught.

11   Is feeling relieved about my mother's death—and then guilt for having felt relief—my own personal, intimate, psychological issue? Is it totally unrelated to the public sphere?

In part, I'd say, "Yes, it's my own problem." No one should feel obligated to take an interest in my personal drama. But, on the other hand, isn't this relief, this burdensome peace, a thorn that no one wants to acknowledge? Isn't it a form of suffering that millions in the world have experienced and still experience whenever they're forced into needing someone they love to die? Isn't this, perhaps, an invisible yet pervasive institution of our modern world?

I remember a conversation about this that took place in a hillside home in Lima, with a woman whose hair was already gray at forty years old. While frying fish, she grunted, "I wish that he would just die already so that we can rest. I wish the damn guy would just leave us in peace." She was surrounded by her children, who were all seated at the Sunday dinner table. I was a guest. The woman's husband was in jail.

For those who've never experienced the misfortune of having someone close to them detained, the acronyms DIRCOTE and DINCOTE probably mean very little—or maybe they just seem like part of the everyday vocabulary people use to talk about political violence in Peru. They're terms that get bandied about all the time in everyday speech. But these terms are like pathways; if you go down them, they conjure experiences that lead to so many more words, sensations, or even smells that make them tangible. For detainees and their families, words like DINCOTE mean torment, fear, lawyers, pleas for help, desperation for someone to pull strings. They mean torture and knowing: knowing that they're torturing your family member. They evoke blood and uncertainty. And when this kind of experience happens repeatedly, DINCOTE, like so many other state-sponsored agencies and secret police organizations that have operated around the world at different points in history (like the Naval School of Mechanics in Argentina or the National Intelligence Directorate in Chile), becomes part of a routine and a nightmare.[1] Walking these paths wears down detainees' loved ones.

Delivering something to a detained family member in prison; getting someone to pass your family member a note, some clothes, some medicine, some food; preventing their disappearance: these things bring solace.

It was this kind of absolute, vicious torment that snuffed out young Eliézer's ability ever to enjoy life again. Following a long battle to sur-

---

1. Escuela de Mecánica de la Armada (Naval School of Mechanics, was a notorious detention and torture center during Argentina's dictatorship (1976–1983). Dirección de Inteligencia Nacional (National Intelligence Directorate, 1973–1977) was General Augusto Pinochet's first secret police organization during the Chilean dictatorship (1973–1990).

vive, Eliézer's father died just a few days after the detention camp where he was being held was liberated. It was as if Eliézer were channeling the words of Elie Wiesel: "I did not weep. It pained me that I could not weep, but I had no more tears. And, in the depths of my being, in the recesses of my weakened conscience . . . I might perhaps have found something like—free at last!"[2]

So this relief, this guilt, this burden that you feel when someone you love finally dies, is not just a personal matter. It's a side effect of impotence and fear, a sign of affect's failure in the face of brute reason. Thousands of families around the world suffer this fate, this dilemma born out of love. And love should, in fact, be part of the public sphere, especially when love is terrible.[3]

12 It doesn't smell like her. It's her moment to shine, and it no longer smells like her. And she had such a particular scent.

The flowers, the signs, the coffee, people greeting one another: she would have hated all of it. But here she is, subjected to the whole family, to a sham ritual acted out by people who grudgingly loved her.

She died just last night, but she already seems like an abandoned corpse, as if touched by a decrepit and tired death.

Right next to me, someone mutters her name. It's strange because people talk about her as if she were an alien, something foreign, a plague.

I'd like to leave, but convention dictates that I stay. So, I stand in the corner observing what I perceive to be a theatrical troupe improvising blindness: they don't see her wounds, her crushed nose, her broken fin-

---

2. Wiesel, *Night Trilogy*, 130.

3. Elie Wiesel's novel and Primo Levi's narratives are unavoidable catalogs of horror, but even more so of the ways in which common men become evil and lose their souls. Survivor guilt becomes a distinguishing mark. How can one speak gravely about modest suffering in the face of horror? What does one gain by showing off minor scratches in a sea of wounds far older than oneself? The history of horror leaves us tongue-tied when we try to tell our own little dramas. But we know: there can't really be scales of suffering because each experience is unique and a body gets destroyed only once. Yes, we know that. But people feel something like shame in sharing their experiences with those who truly suffered.

gers. She died of death—that's all! Her blood stains are shrouded in secrets, and by the jokes people tell at wakes, and by the blue doilies strewn about the room.

There she lies, drying up like an awkward mummy.

It might seem like I'm crazy, but at that moment I know . . . I know . . . I know that by some force of inertia her body is still repeating what she was dreaming yesterday—when defeated and exhausted by torture she dreamed of death. I can't stand it. I want her to get up. I want all these people to leave, to leave us alone. I'd love to have the courage to scream, "Get out of here! Cut the charade! I know you're all happy now: the 'dead woman walking' is really dead! The cursed one, the terrorist, the bitch—is dead! At long last! You don't have to be afraid anymore! So, get out of here! There's no need to wait around to see if she comes back to life!"

But I do nothing. I just look at her there dreaming in echoes.

Like an idiot, a coward, I close my eyes to see if by magic I can locate her in the darkness—to see if in my mind I can sing a song to her on a Paraguayan lagoon, or promise her that I'll be all that she dreamed I'd be.

But there's no magic here. There's nothing more than noise in this room, and this heat, and hands patting me on the back. It's absurd, I know. I know. But I still feel. I feel. I move toward the exit with my eyes closed. I manage to avoid condolences, and arms, and sweat. And I search for her.

But I don't find her. Not yet. So we can rest. So that she never again has to dream that dream, or any other. So that for once she can be just like any other normal person.

So she can rot. In peace.

13 I met him on one of the trips I took while working for the TRC. We visited many communities back then. They were all similar, each full of nearly carbon-copy stories. Women would stand in long lines to give their testimonies. The men and the authorities would tell their official stories. But occasionally something unique would happen: an authentic moment that would undo the spell cast by such tough work.

Maybe it happened because we were more or less the same age. Maybe it was because I told him some things privately, or because I gave him a book. I don't know. Juan showed me the graves where they had buried both the Shining Path militants and his neighbors who had joined Shining Path. It was the community secret. They had killed those neighbors to prove to the military that *they* were not *terrucos*.

But proof is not enough. War has its own logic and breeds so many complex situations. The army tortured and executed fifteen townsmen on the public square; they took others away and killed them in a nearby village. And they did this because they "knew" that those people were terrucos, terrorists, and that despite any argument to the contrary, the community had been a base of operations for Shining Path.

Juan tells me that reparations aren't that important to them, that they'll be fine, but that above all they want one thing. He asks me to request that the TRC help them reconcile with their brothers from the Ichu community, so that the Ichu will forgive them. The rest of his *compañeros*, the community leadership, agree: let the TRC help us.

My comrades and I get ready to push on to another community along our route. But just as our truck is about to leave, Juan insists. His Spanish is perfect, almost urban. He has an anxious look on his face, as if his chance were slipping away, only to be lost among piles of documents and testimonies. "Please, let the TRC help us convince our neighbors to forgive us. Help them understand that many of us were forced to do it—or that we did it without knowing much. I was just a kid back when Shining Path made us kill our neighbors. Ever since then, the Ichu hate us. And we've repented."

Juan walks for a while alongside the truck. I don't know exactly what to say to him. I understand that he needs peace, that his conscience needs calming. Knowing that other people justifiably hate him doesn't keep him from living, yet it marks him. I say something to him, spout off some formulaic response culled from the lexicon of human rights. But I know that they're just useless words.

14 Words make it repeatedly clear: they were terrorists, criminals, assassins, the worst thing that has happened to this country in all its history. The TRC is clear about this, too: the main group responsible for the Internal Armed Conflict was the Peruvian Communist Party–Shining Path, which declared war on the Peruvian state and caused the greatest number of deaths, the majority of them Quechua-speaking indigenous people. It was the worst bloodbath in the republic's history.[4]

I chat with a couple of former Shining Path militants who are now part of MOVADEF. They admit to certain errors, but they have justifications for their actions at the ready. They've had years to work out those justifications while in prison. How can we blame them? They have to go on living somehow. They can't survive with a past that brings them only shame. Their personal stories must be saved from disgrace.

One guy pounces on me. He says we should go to the prison on Sunday because there's someone there who was with my father when he died—right up to the end—and he has something to tell me. I tell him I'll think about it. Then he invites me to write something for a journal he publishes. I tell him it's not a bad idea, and I give him a few copies of the poetry book I wrote.

Former Shining Path militants don't believe anything that discredits them. They don't believe in the TRC or the NGOs. They tell a bunch of highly detailed anecdotes to prove that the massacres attributed to Shining Path were really perpetrated by the army. "We wouldn't have been so dumb as to do that!" they say. They even downplay a major event such as the Tarata Street car bombing, which happened right in the heart of Lima's Miraflores neighborhood; they call those killings a stroke of incredibly bad luck. "The explosion shouldn't have happened in a residential building; it should have happened nearby at the bank. That was the worst thing that could have happened to us," they say, annoyed. I mention the death of the Afro-Peruvian feminist and community organizer María Elena Moyano, her body treated with terrible scorn. They acknowledge that her death was an excess, an error, but say that she deserved it. "Everything they say is a lie. We didn't kill like they did, like the reactionaries did!"[5]

---

4. These were the first and main conclusions of the TRC and were detailed in its Final Report.

5. The Tarata bombing and the assassination of María Elena Moyano are the two best-known terrorist acts that Shining Path committed in Lima. These events showed the capital's inhabitants just how brutal the group's actions were. On Tarata Street, in the residential neighborhood of Miraflores, Shining Path placed explosives that practically turned a building into rubble, leaving twenty-five dead and 155 wounded. They killed Moyano, a notable leader within the legal Peruvian Left, in front of her children and in her own neighborhood, Villa El Salvador. They later blew up her body with dynamite.

Even though I didn't plan to do it, I calmly tell them, as if reciting from memory, about my own experience working with the TRC. I tell them briefly, but with lots of examples, that Shining Path *did* kill and that the killing *was* terribly brutal. They can choose not to believe the TRC, but why won't they believe me or the people who told me about what Shining Path did? The quieter of the two guys replies, "We didn't know much about what was going on in the countryside." Then the other one adds, "You might be right, but we'd have to verify what you're saying."

The two guys leave happy. They've also recorded my voice, astutely, and they can take that recording of us wherever they want. It's obvious that they want to talk, to speak out, even to be questioned, but by someone who understands something of the language they speak, of the pressures they feel, of their grief.

I stay there thinking for quite a while, doubting if I should write about this encounter or share it in my blog or on the internet. I decide not to share it, like the majority of my writings. I can't sit down, take an objective distance, so I simply describe this conversation that took place over coffee as if it were any old Lima scene.

What's missing is my part. And I'm not sure if I'm ready to express it clearly. Shining Path's brand of justification doesn't do me any good: their rhetorical escape mechanisms, their ideological formulas, their discrediting of the NGOs and the TRC. I've worked with those groups. I've been a human rights activist since I was really young, and I've been so wholeheartedly.

I know it's true: I know that the thousands of atrocities that Shining Path committed as the cost of carrying out its revolution are real. I know that the end was foreseeable, that the revolution blinded Shining Path and made the group prioritize the future good over the present good. I know that they were sick with hunger for justice—that an excessive hunger for justice drove them to hatred, and that a thirst for change drove them to destruction. Perhaps the MRTA leader Alberto Gálvez Olaechea said it best, even though he wasn't a Senderista himself: "We wanted change immediately."[6] That's what defined Shining Path, I think, at least partially.

---

6. Alberto Gálvez Olaechea was an MRTA leader who was released in 2015. In his book, *Desde el país de las sombras* (2009), and even before , Gálvez has constructed a

I know that my parents were part of that world. I know that during the operation in which my father was detained for the last time, a police officer was killed. I don't know if my father fired the shot. It's hard for me to imagine. But I also believe that it could have been possible. My father was a decisive, courageous guy. But that police officer was a poor man, a worker who assuredly got frightened while chasing the car in which my father and his comrades were fleeing. The bullet must have hurt him, burned him, paralyzed him while he thought about his family, as his short, twenty-something-year-old life slipped away.

The police officer's family no longer has him by their side. They're just a widow and orphans. Like us. How can I ask their forgiveness? Should I ask their forgiveness?

15 I'm sure of it now. It wasn't just us, her children, who implored my mother to get out of the country. Everyone knew they were going to kill her. Many of those around her had died or been detained. Police and army vigilance became sloppy and scandalous. Intelligence agents would barge into our little store at the University of San Marcos; brazenly, they would eye us up and down and then leave. They'd even come dressed in uniform. One afternoon, a tall, burly guy showed up wearing a light gray uniform. He saw us. My mother was seated there typing some student's homework on her old typewriter, and I was standing next to her, dictating. The guy said something like, "Yeah, it's her." We shot him a look, and then he left.

Some of her close friends, the ones who weren't involved in the Party, also warned her to get out of the country. A good, young man, a very dear friend who was part of Shining Path but who had the foresight to get out before they killed him, also advised her to go. "Flaca, why are you still involved in this shit? It doesn't make sense anymore. You know that." That young man managed to get out of the country; he's still alive, and we still love him from afar, but we don't contact him.

---

discourse in which he takes responsibility for what he did during the years of political violence and takes distance from the motivations and methods to which he subscribed in what he calls his fervor to change things and combat social injustice. His testimony and reflection are important because they aren't simple: they're imperfect, they contain arguments and counterarguments, and they're painstakingly constructed. However, he hasn't yet found interlocutors willing to make the same, equally imperfect effort to communicate.

Some friends of my mother's friends who worked for an NGO and who knew her from her days in the legalized, radical Left, before she joined Shining Path, also told her to go. They held her in high regard and, despite their political differences, offered to help her find a way out. Some of our family members encouraged her to leave, too. But she'd respond to them with few words, asking them to make sure her children were cared for, to make sure nothing happened to them.

Some of my mother's Party comrades accused her of preferring to raise children instead of giving herself fully to the revolution. She didn't pay them any mind. The problems she faced, for years, because she chose to raise a family are really complicated; the moment will come to think them through more fully. Whenever I would ask her to leave—at every chance I got, every so often—she'd simply smile and say, "Don't worry about it." Then she'd say things like, "What's going to become of you kids?" That would infuriate me. I'd tell her that we were all grown up and that we'd know what to do.

In the end, she never left. Instead, she wound up paralyzed on a Chorrillos beach, riddled with three bullets. It's in that same place where I still envision her, serene, her blood mingling with the ocean, in a scene that plays back in my mind on loop.

For a long time, I've been fighting the guilty feeling that comes from thinking that my mother exposed herself to a lot of risk for her children. Even in the worst moments that our family experienced during the war, the times were few and far between when she'd leave to seek a safe haven. She'd always come back, find work, and put food on the table for us. The police would locate us, come to our house, wake us up, point her out, root through our meager belongings, our clothes, our books. They'd threaten to take her away, but they wouldn't do it. I'm not sure why. Then we'd go to another house, at least for a while. My mother became the target of much criticism: "Leave the kids, and go into hiding! Abandon the shitty P, and flee the country."[7]

---

7. Shining Path's members could be quite different from one another, constructing their militancy with their own baggage, characteristics, needs, and margin for action. To think of Shining Path militants only as bloodthirsty, vengeful beings, or as unknowable, deprives us of the chance to understand better a time that still touches the present. Research such as Asencios's *La ciudad acorralada* (2017) helps our understanding.

I know that with her decision not to abandon us and to participate in the revolution part-time, she was watching over us, but at the same time her decision left us exposed. Both of these things were true. She couldn't avoid it. She thought it necessary to change the world that left her indignant and distressed. But she couldn't simply abandon us and let us become poorer than we already were.

I've thought about my mother for years. Why didn't she leave? I think that, at least in part, it was because of her children. We didn't ask her to stay. We didn't want that guilt. And we told her so.

But I also think she didn't leave because she just couldn't do it—not just because of us, but because of inertia, in part, and also because she couldn't imagine surrendering her life in such a monumental way. I knew her deeply. I know that she was like an open book—that she loved people, perhaps too much, if that's possible. She felt other people's pain to the point of suffering. By the early 1990s, she knew that Shining Path was a terrible mistake. But she couldn't get out completely. Being part of that world was the only thing that gave sense to her life.

She wasn't ready to surrender.

16   Shining Path killed thousands of people. Before they died, thousands of them were terribly mistreated. After they died, hundreds or perhaps thousands of their bodies were used as public spectacles, as part of a pedagogy of fear. We can still feel the war's consequences in towns, in neighborhoods, in politics, in institutions.

Children shouldn't inherit their parents' guilt. It's unjust. But they inherit it all the same, because justice is little more than a word. Justice has to be built through every human exchange. It's not a categorical imperative.

When my well-intentioned colleagues talk about Shining Path's monstrousness, I agree with them. But I know, at the same time, that they're talking about my family—and about lots of friends whom I saw live fully and later die. It's hard for me to remember those friends as monsters. But, yes, they committed atrocities, and, yes, they justified them.

When other concerned colleagues point out that something must be done to detain and keep tabs on Shining Path militants once they've been let out of prison, I basically agree with them because I understand their fears and anxiety—and because I know enough about the people who are being let out to assume that they'll organize again and will seek new political roles.

But I also know that when we study situations in detail, we uncover hidden meanings that grand narratives and fear tend to eclipse. I'm trying to say that the monsters from Shining Path may have had motivations for acting as they did—and those motivations could have changed over time. They also could have suffered in ways that were far from banal. In reality, within each monster is another thousand-headed monster, a complete fauna or bestiary. Every Senderista had his or her way of being in Sendero, and all Senderistas existed in tension with the institution that was Shining Path.

To restore substance to their lives, to put them in context, or to recover their life trajectories or their generational experience doesn't mean justifying their crimes or promoting revisionism.[8] I also don't believe it's simply about restoring their humanity. Rather, it's about taking a hard look at who Shining Path's militants really were. It's about looking at them deeply and head-on to get to know who they were as real people in society. If you want to restore something to them—whether it's their humanity or whatever else—that's your own business.

I recently found an example of the complexity I'm talking about in a noteworthy book that circulated only among a select group of people. The author, who prefers to remain anonymous, took years to find an adequate form in which to talk about Shining Path publicly. His research is a kind of vindication. It's work that deserves to be read more than once as a lesson in how to construct a legitimate place from which to speak. It also illustrates how long the road is to become an intellectual—and what the costs are.[9]

---

8. I asked some young anarchists at a meeting in downtown Lima if their desire to "contextualize" Shining Path wasn't an intellectualized strategy for justifying the group's actions. It's difficult to use words like this because they're like traps. Would it help to say that putting Shining Path in context is like casting the group against a background so as to bring its individual faces into relief more clearly and with greater contrast? Doesn't context matter only for seeing oneself better, for scrutinizing an uncovered, exposed face without leniency? But, again, words trap us. No leniency? Is that what we're after?

9. Even now, I won't cite my friend's work, to honor his wishes—because what a person can write in one context and share among friends can be quite uncomfortable to share beyond that inner circle.

In short, we have to get to know Shining Path's militants in ways that go beyond stereotypes. This is because, ultimately, there were Senderistas, lots of them, who weren't puppets, who weren't merely pawns. They were children of their context, yes, but not just by-products of the structures of which they were a part. They decided to risk their lives in a war that no one had declared against them. Don't people and experiences like those deserve intellectuals' serious attention?

Such was the case of my parents and of the people I met from Shining Path. They had their reasons for being leftists, for being radicals like many others were back then. But they also had an extra motivation that was hard to see or apprehend and that fueled only a minority of people: they wanted to take up arms, to fight power with force. And why? The answer to this question always eludes me. It's the question that haunted the historian Carlos Iván Degregori until the end of his life. Carlos Iván once said something like: "That's what we haven't done yet. We haven't understood the people or why they did it. I'm not talking about general explanations. We more or less have those. I'm talking about understanding the people themselves, the Juans and Marías. They're the ones I haven't managed to understand yet."[10] Carlos Iván would get frustrated, like me, like so many others.

When the victims of human rights violations would tell me their stories or describe the resentments they harbored toward the army or Shining Path, when they'd tell me about the harrowing torture they'd suffered at the hands of either of these groups, I would concentrate the entirety of my being on hearing them, on giving them the only capital I possessed: my ability to listen so that they could exist. They and their stories could finally exist in the world because someone had heard them.

After hearing them tell their stories so many times, for years, I never felt like they were talking about my family. I shared their suffering and indignation. I gave all of myself to helping them achieve—if not justice or reparations—at least the passing tranquility of knowing someone had accepted them. One has so little to offer them. But later, later when my work was done, I asked myself: What if they knew my parents had been in Shining Path? Would they have kept telling me their stories? Would they still be my friends?

---

10. Agüero and Sandoval, *Aprendiendo a vivir*, 143, 157.

What would I tell them then? That my parents weren't monsters, that they had their motivations for fighting, that they had ideals, that they had urgent needs? If I told them these things, would that take away my parents' guilt? The devil's advocate could come back at me quite justifiably and ask, "Would these motivations have given your parents and their comrades the right to kill, to shoot, to burn, to break, to destroy?"

I don't think so. Maybe it would have given some sense to their lives. It would have helped to open a place for them in history rather than expel them as outcasts, as if they were a nightmare or a plague. But, finally, my fictitious interlocutor—let's call him the Peruvian rumor mill—might ask me, "Does talking about any of this benefit us in any way? Does it help us heal or bring peace to those left behind? Does it help society?"

Whether this exercise is useful or not is, well, uncertain.

17 Twice I've asked forgiveness on my father's behalf. They were both moments of confusion. It wasn't as if I were harboring an urge to do so in my adolescence or youth. I did it without thinking. A bunch of minor events led me to do it—none of them dramatic. What's more, my attempts at asking forgiveness were clumsy. On one occasion, I blindly wrote an email. The reply I got was cold, but proper. The person said I really had no reason to ask forgiveness, that what happened had nothing to do with me. "Please don't contact us again. Thank you." What did I expect him to say? Doing this didn't make me feel better or worse. It just made me feel ridiculous.

18 I sent some other emails back then to people who I knew had shared experiences with my father. I tacked on some formula like, "If my father caused you any harm or damage, I ask your forgiveness in his name." I received only two replies. One of them said, "Your father and mother did a lot of harm to my family. I'm writing to you on my father's behalf because he doesn't know how to use email. We kindly request that you not communicate with us anymore. May peace be with your family." The second one said something to the effect of, "Your father was a great friend. I have very fond memories of him and your mother. But it's out of place for you to ask forgiveness in his name. Affectionately yours."

The first reply made me think about that son, a man obviously bothered by my message and who lived his childhood in anguish because his family had been part of my parents' circle of influence. They bred anguish within that circle, like a contagion of danger. They did it by asking favors of people, by asking them to store things, or by asking the most committed ones to give other Senderistas lodging or food. They'd use a kind of blackmail, saying, "You're either with us or against us." Or, "If you don't do what we're asking, you're just like all the rest of them—just blowing smoke." I can only imagine the fear they felt when those they were harboring got captured or when they saw on the news that my parents were in jail. They'd be thinking, "Now they're coming for us," or, "We're going to lose our jobs." The son's response made me feel as if I had no right to keep bothering him about the past. It was a mistake.

The second reply made me feel ashamed. The woman who wrote back to me is a beautiful soul, someone capable of putting herself in another's shoes easily, without drama, someone who had also done her fair share of suffering. Her response to me was an embrace. When I received it, it made me think that I shouldn't have been so clumsy and naive, so out of touch. It was a matter of pride. There are embraces whose warmth leaves us naked. I would have preferred not to write anything nor to receive any response.

Words, they come and go. In the end, they cease to mean anything. They'll be forgotten. Knowing that allowed me to forgive myself. But then I said to myself, "I'll never ask forgiveness again."

I'm breaking that promise now. But to ask forgiveness in this way is my right—not a form of humiliation.

19 I once wrote, "Children shouldn't inherit their parents' guilt. It's unjust." But, of course, they do. Guilt is complex. It takes many forms. It adapts because communities feel a need to blame someone.

My parents' actions caused a series of chain reactions that continue to this day. Because they touched many lives, they affected people's paths forever, mostly for ill.

My parents' actions were diverse: they killed, they prepared attacks, they exposed women and men to harm, they weakened union and local leadership, and they affected families and their dynamics. My parents' "work with the masses," which I saw in action on more than one occasion, was like skilled seduction: they instilled hope for change in impressionable people. They'd introduce the P, little by little, like a secret entity, but whose presence could be felt, whose effects were real. To support the combatants' work, that of the "people's finest sons," was seen as an act of great solidarity, generous and selfless, the best thing one could do because things really worth doing involved risk.

Like a virus—that's how my parents acted! That's how lots of humble women suddenly found themselves caught up in an enormous war game that went far beyond their comprehension. What happened to the people who were seduced? Where did they wind up? Where did they hide? What fears did they have to face?

The effects of my parents' actions didn't end with their deaths. The leftist girl who fell in love with my father after he was in prison, the one who later became his girlfriend, affected her family. She wound up in jail, too. Her children suffered because of her choices. Señora Sara, who helped my mother in the worst of times, had to flee our neighborhood, leaving her children poorly tended. One of them, "the Twin," became a criminal and is now dead.

I don't think these people were puppets (so many come to mind—the woman who made sausages and potatoes, my father's coworker, the kids from school). They didn't allow themselves to be manipulated clumsily. But my parents did intrude in their lives decisively. They were like activators: they tapped people whose skin was already sensitive to the touch. And what they brought with them was bad: death in the worst cases (as with Miguel and Juan, both rebellious kids, happy and full of energy), incarceration or uprooting from home in other cases (as with Héctor, an enormously talented physicist).

I remember the rage that one of my university classmates, a history student like me, felt toward a very erudite professor, who was a political extremist, and toward others like him. There were so many leftist extremists like that professor who, through their words and influence, indoctrinated their students and inspired them to terrible radicalization. The students then joined Shining Path, only to die, disappear, or rot in jail. The teachers lingered in their students' lives as provocateurs and radical thinkers.

So many other leftist leaders fit this description! Many touted the language of revolution, the imperative to change, an awareness of injustice and indignity (an inability to live peacefully as long as injustice pervaded every aspect of daily life). They preached the option to take courage and dare to fight with force. This is how they nourished sensitive and rebellious souls. To toy with young people in this way pushed them to the brink of an extreme decision. And many made that decision.

Leftist leaders did not make the same decision. Some of them kept irresponsibly preaching armed struggle until the destruction of the United Left destroyed them, too. We should forgive them as well. They were children of their times. They've now been defeated. And although some of them still walk around public squares and write in newspapers, they haven't yet realized how ghostlike they've become.

III. Ancestors

Today I remember the dead in my house.
The woman who died night after night
and her dying was a long good-bye,
a train that never left.

Octavio Paz, "Interrupted Elegy"

20 A few years back, a well-known journalist wrote a short text about my father that circulated on the internet. He described some moments they shared in their youth: a job they did in the central highlands that ended poorly because they had abusive bosses. He mentioned my father's leftist militancy, his role as a union leader during the massive protests and national strikes of the late 1970s. He also remembered when my father died in 1986 on El Frontón prison island, along with a hundred other prisoners, all of them accused of belonging to Shining Path.[1]

When the journalist evoked my father's memory, he described him as a man who'd been true to his convictions, a courageous guy. He sensed a certain continuity between how my father acted when he was a young

---

1. For a report on the case, see Comisión de la Verdad, *Informe final*, 7:234–263. It's probable that 122 prisoners died at El Frontón. Beyond the judicial realm, it has become quite clear that the chain of responsibility that led to the extrajudicial killings of the surrendered prisoners in the Blue Pavilion of the Prison Island goes all the way up to the highest authorities, including then-president of the republic, Alan García.

man—defending his coworkers from their abusive bosses and even risking his own job—and the man who, as far as he'd heard, was one of the last to make his way out of the destroyed cellblock and was later shot to death.

The journalist's column sparked a flurry of emails, but I especially remember one written in a morally superior tone. A human rights and transitional justice professional responded to the column arguing that there was no need to go searching for heroes among delinquents and terrorists; it would be better, he thought, to seek heroes among the civilian victims. He even went so far as to suggest that the journalist was amoral.

I admit that it's reasonable to agree with the transitional justice professional. But, at the same time, I think his reasoning is sterile and far too wrapped up in its own worth. I acknowledge that I'm not an objective party: I'm the son of the terrorist that the transitional justice professional was treating like dirt. Yet I still suspect that his impenetrable line of reasoning is a screen that blocks out the real questions we should be asking, covering them up with easy truths and comfortable consensus.

Is it possible for Shining Path terrorists to die with dignity? Is it possible for them to die concerned about their wounded comrades, attempting to save them? Can they die in silence, without groveling to their killers, instead standing tall in front of them? Is it possible to eke out even a shred of dignity from the agony of those who lived for so long feeling like they were being crushed under the weight of a wall, any insignificant shred of dignity that might remain in this country that's suffered so much?

Yes, of course we should recognize that heroes and heroines exist among those killed by Shining Path or the armed forces. They should come first when we talk about courage, honor, or solidarity. But once we've doled out our thanks to all of them, isn't there anything left for anyone else?

Does having sinned make sinners repugnant? Does it alienate them from the human race? Should it set them apart from the elite group of perfect human beings? Can we find only malice in every act of Shining Path? Are those who belonged to that group somehow more imperfect than all the other imperfect beings that fill our past and present?

Maybe they are. Maybe their barbarity was extreme, so extreme that they gave up their membership card in the human race. When we think about those who oversaw the Nazi concentration camps, it's natural for us to feel like they have nothing to do with us. But is this really true? Always? Is it true of all Senderistas? Do they really have nothing to do with us?

Today, anyone who had a friend in Shining Path can't remember that person affectionately in public. It's not ethically acceptable for people who belonged to Shining Path to possess human qualities. A child can't be proud of a parent's horrendous death or of any of the infinite possible ways that parent could have died. The family story stays frozen in time.

Should we start over again?

21 My ancestors are cursed. They aren't innocent. They waged war, their wretched war. They brought tragedy to so many. They died, astray, in a war of their own making.

In our family, we never cast ourselves as victims. My mother taught us not to do that. In her mind, my father died in combat. She demanded his body be given back to her, yet he remains disappeared to this day. She felt indignation, not because he died but because of how a group of surrendered prisoners was massacred.

When our mother died later on, executed like my father, we children never felt like victims. We never raised much of a fuss about either of them. We buried them in a rush, amid tension and poverty.

Children of terrorists have no right to grandiose displays of mourning. Everything, including death, is part of a transparent and vulgar secret.[2]

---

2. It's all so vulgar. In 2004, the Public Ministry informed us that it had managed to identify my father's remains and those of thirty others killed at El Frontón. They negligently and clumsily gathered all the families in a dusty room filled with boxes. Supported by dear friends, forensic specialists whom we asked about the discovery, we refused to accept the remains without lodging further complaints. Our friends categorially stated that the whole thing was a farce: that it was technically impossible to identify remains in such conditions. But it was sad to see how some family members, despite the obvious farce, still took the boxes home with them. It didn't seem to matter to them if their loved ones' remains were really in there. They needed them. Now they've buried them somewhere and can go visit them. They can finally take flowers to someone who for so many years was disappeared—only it isn't their loved one. They're just remains, remains of people like anyone else. Why add insult to injury and make a mockery of it all?

22   The president of Uruguay, José Mujica, thinks that the Uruguayan dictatorship's crimes shouldn't be investigated because he and his comrades who suffered repression were combatants, not victims. He has blocked the attempts of human rights activists to abolish the amnesty law that exists in his country.

I understand Mujica's perspective. I understand his discourse and, perhaps, even more than his discourse, his wager. He's trading a nonnegotiable right—like the right to life and integrity—to secure peace.

But I also understand those who suffer because of Mujica's decision, those who argue that the Tupamaros have rights that should be respected whether or not they were combatants, those who believe that even though the Tupamaros are dead or disappeared, their status as militants, former guerrillas, or guilty people doesn't abolish their right or their families' right to justice and reparations. What's more, Mujica is sacrificing others along with himself: families who don't agree with his vocation for peace or his strategies for governance. His actions are an abuse of his position.

It doesn't matter if I don't feel like a victim and if I've never behaved like one. The fact is: if this world of norms and morals in which we live has any value, then I am a victim—whether or not I wish to be.

23   Parents who bury their children . . . It's often said that to break the natural cycle, to bury a child, is one of life's worst fates. My grandmother visited her son in jail. She brought him food, clothing. She sometimes took his kids to visit him. What did she think of him? He had been her darling child. She chalked up his militancy in the Peruvian Left and later in Shining Path to my mother's influence.

In June 1986, when my father died in prison—such an awful place full of nerves, fear, and rage—my grandmother refused to accept that her son was dead. She paid no attention to what we told her, even though we gave her details whenever she asked for them.[3] She didn't want to be-

---

3. Shining Path took these sorts of things "seriously." For a case as complicated as that of my father's death, they gave us very detailed and rigorous information. They told us when he came out of the pavilion alive, how he was identified as a delegate and then tortured, when he was shot, who killed him, and which prisoner was the "traitor" who informed on him. I've always thought about that "traitor." My mother told me that the

El Frontón, a prison island off the port of Callao, where José Manuel Agüero Aguirre and at least one hundred other Shining Path prisoners were killed in June 1986. The prison was subsequently razed. Photo by Virginia Rojas, 2018. Courtesy of the artist.

lieve it even days later, when the survivors' testimonies became known. My grandmother went to meetings and demanded that those responsible hand over the bodies, that they clarify what had happened. She hated doing it, but she went anyway.

I remember her sitting there, trying to recognize her son in a newspaper photo that showed only a mangled, blurry handful of survivors. She saw him. It was he! She knew him by his long legs, his boots. It was he! But it wasn't.

She laid out her son's clothing beneath his photograph, as if it were a wake. She cried for years. She dreamed of him so many times. She dreamed of him telling her jokes, because he was her little white boy, her

marines shot him after they used him. I am disturbed by his desperation, his fear of death, and his willingness to use any tool at his disposal as capital to survive. To stay alive, he had nothing to give other than his honor, his own comrades, his memory, his words. Words didn't save him in the end.

José Carlos Agüero visiting El Frontón, where his father and more than one hundred other prisoners were killed in June 1986. Photo by Virginia Rojas, 2018. Courtesy of the artist.

blanquito, the *criollo*, the promise. She dreamed of him saying to her, "I'm alive. Come find me, Mamá."

I remember the day she told us that she saw him in her window, the one with the broken pane. She saw his foot extend through the glass. It was absurd and ugly. And he said to her, "Don't suffer any more, Mamá. Look how I am."

That dream disturbed her.

She was a hardened woman, quite hardened. She had raised her kids alone. She'd migrated from Tarma to Lima. She'd sent all her kids to college. And now her little boy returned to her in dreams to ask her to let him rest in peace.

I avoided her for a long time. I was put off by her scent, which was like firewood. I didn't like that she saw me as a clone of my father. She'd ask me to sit next to her and tell her whatever popped into my mind. But her process never wavered. Ultimately, she always saw him in me. And she'd cry. And she'd caress me. And her tears wouldn't move me; they'd make me uncomfortable.

I wanted to think about something else. That's why I stopped seeing her for a time. I had to survive, and with her I couldn't. Later she fell prey to quickly progressing dementia. But when I'd go visit her, she'd still recognize me. Or she recognized someone else, invoked.

24   A symbol can be worth a lot! My grandmother hated Shining Path, and she hated my mother, the terrorist who had sweet-talked her son and led him down the path to death. Nevertheless, she attended a tribute that Sendero organized at the University of San Marcos Medical School for those who had disappeared or died in the prison massacres. With confused pride, she received a little pin, a brooch in memory of the dead. She saved it.

She never could bury her son's body, and that left her tremendously damaged. But she appreciated that act of acknowledgment, that symbol, that ceremony put together by the very terrorists who had steered her little boy toward his death.

She hated Alan García, who was president of Peru during the prison massacres, as if he were her personal enemy. She hated my mother, too, for so many years. But Alan García was the devil to her. She never forgave him. She eventually managed to forgive my mother—and, later, to love her.

IV. Accomplices

We are waiting for the rain to stop,
although we have got accustomed
to standing behind the curtain, being invisible.

Günter Grass, "The Flood"

25 I had already written most of these vignettes when I read Lurgio Gavilán Sánchez's *Memorias de un soldado desconocido* (2012; published in English as *When Rains Became Floods: A Child Soldier's Story*, 2015). People had told me about his noteworthy life. Carlos Iván Degregori, an enthusiast of Lurgio's to the end, predicted that Gavilán's book would be a hit. And it has been. I think it has been, among other reasons, because Lurgio's discourse—that of a child in Shining Path who became a soldier in the Peruvian army as an adolescent, a priest as a young man, and an anthropologist as an adult—is the type of discourse that some of the Peruvian people were waiting to hear, especially people from Ayacucho. Gavilán is their interpreter, their prophet. He's like Salieri from Milos Forman's *Amadeus*, a kind of patron saint, though not of the mediocre, but rather of those who were collectively stigmatized.[1]

---

1. In the final scene of this 1984 film, the composer Antonio Salieri, the patron saint of mediocre people, blesses the alienated, the dregs of society, from his wheelchair in an asylum, as he awaits death.

Gavilán's book has helped people from Ayacucho feel exonerated. It also helps them to find a rationale for things that, in Ayacucho, are common knowledge: namely, that so many people supported Sendero, that everyone in the communities supported the group, and that people later internalized Shining Path's doctrine of total war and, in many cases, had to kill to survive. By now, however, the myth of the innocent community has become untenable. So, it has to be replaced by another myth: that of a community stripped of its pastoral bliss and born into a world of pain.

Gavilán uses several strategies to accomplish this. He narrates through a child's eyes, infantilizing war and taking on the attributes of a child, mostly naivete and innocence. He also resorts to conservative discourse, claiming that indigenous people like him lacked the tools to understand Shining Path's manuals and the complexities of political life. He wants to be treated like an indigenous man from Uchuraccay. He wants Mario Vargas Llosa to write about him.[2]

At every turn, Gavilán avoids creating moments of tension that might call his morality into question. And that's not by chance. Everything—even a scene of mass rape—becomes a funny or futile occurrence. Yes, Gavilán complains about things, but mainly about how annoyed he feels that abusive army leaders made cadets like him pay extra for sexual favors from indigenous women. He doesn't narrate sexual violence as a dramatic plot twist, but rather as mere anecdote.

---

2. This alludes to the "Vargas Llosa Report" that investigated the massacre of journalists in Uchuraccay, a highland community of Huanta, in January 1983, a noteworthy and key event of the period. The conclusions of the Comisión Investigadora de los Sucesos de Uchuraccay, led by Mario Vargas Llosa, proved largely correct and were confirmed by the TRC in 2003. However, the commission presented a cultural interpretation of the peasants who killed the journalists, describing them as premodern, in need of tutelage because the complexity of the war was too much for them. But it should be pointed out that Vargas Llosa fulfilled this task without any obligation to do so. He was already a world-renowned writer, yet he took on the challenge with devotion, stoicism, and admirable civic responsibility. We have the images of him a few years later, standing for hours and declaring to a provincial judge. In the midst of the war, in an Andean world that he did not know and considered backward, his sense of republican duty, of collaborating to clarify the events and with the administration of justice, is admirable. But the public memory of these massacres' history, the history of human rights in Peru, does not recognize him for this. That's because it is a field dominated by the Left.

Can we expect anything more from an author with such a complicated past, from someone who, despite his limitations, dares to speak in the first person about the role he played in the war? Does any space for free speech exist in which Gavilán could really think deeply about his level of commitment to the war and its crimes, in which he wouldn't have to worry about striking just the right tone or risk paying a social or even judicial price for speaking out? That space doesn't yet exist. But if Gavilán's book contributes anything—however little or however much— it's that he lays the groundwork, a cornerstone, for greater degrees of free speech. Let us hope we won't just stay stuck where we are, fulfilling Manuel Scorza's truism that Peru consistently has had a hard time laying anything more than cornerstones.[3]

26   During the conflict, a well-known NGO provided humanitarian aid to United Left prisoners and also, indirectly, to Shining Path. The NGO knew quite well whom it was supporting. But perhaps a general sense of humanity prevented it from simply saying, "We're not going to help these prisoners at all."

That same NGO helped various people get out of the country because it knew that they were at risk of being killed or disappeared for belonging to Shining Path. My own mother, who knew the NGO workers from their shared days as leftist militants, remained close to them for many years, coordinating small gestures of support such as clothing or food. Although the NGO was careful about what it was doing and didn't support Shining Path politically, it also didn't turn its back on the human needs of Sendero militants. How could they deny aid to their old friends, to people with whom they shared many ideas and a sense of common purpose?

The NGO workers argued with my mother, begging her to leave the country because they knew she would certainly be killed if she stayed. But they never managed to convince her. It's easy to point a finger at the NGOs for not cutting ties with Shining Path, for letting themselves be used as sounding boards or "willing fools." I think, however, that many of them did, in fact, cut ties early on. The legal units of the NGOs, for ex-

---

3. Scorza, introduction to *Redoble por Rancas*.

ample, took the initiative not to sponsor any Shining Path militant. They sponsored only innocent victims.

But who is innocent, and of what? That's indeed much harder to define. Marie Manrique has meticulously argued that innocence and guilt are discursive, political, and tactical constructions.[4] They're identities that accused people develop laboriously when opportunity and context permit. They're also labels that are imposed from the outside by NGOs, churches, the state, and other actors. In other words, innocence is more than just a matter of actually being innocent or seeming innocent. It's a social practice that we can reconstruct. More than fixed identities, guilt and innocence stem from a set of decisions made about a person's identity.

One way of telling the story of Peru's NGOs is to focus on how they shirked their responsibility to defend everyone equally—human rights are, in fact, nonnegotiable—and instead defended only the innocent, forsaking all others and using a set of exclusionary criteria. In this case, those deemed guilty were sent off to be tortured, jailed, disappeared, or killed. That's undoubtedly part of the truth. But I prefer that this story be more than a mere deconstruction of NGOs' ethically inconsistent practices. It doesn't seem fair to focus only on that. I prefer to sum things up like this: If what we need to defend life and liberty—in a context where there are really no good options—is to hold certain people up to the light as innocent, then let's do that.

Constructing innocence has merit. It's sadly meritorious and obviously a resistance strategy, a strategy of the weak. By creating innocent victims, the NGOs did the most possible good they could in a desperate situation. But, yes, they also left all of the guilty on their own.

Torture, the rape of guilty prisoners, impunity . . . Certain indefensible, unnameable actors became social taboo, people devoid of rights. They were the ones whom we had to block out of our field of vision so that we could keep on working, even though we saw them there suffering in horrifying prison cells, even though their right to due process had been violated, even though they weren't released from prison after they'd served out their sentences. To look the other way, to stay blind—that's the price our rights-based community had to pay to get things accomplished in the midst of a terrible war.

---

4. Manrique, "Generando la inocencia," 70–71.

To this day, we still can't talk about this. Human rights reached their limit: defeated, impotent, surrendered.

27   A dear friend, who in the mid-1980s was really up to speed on what was going on, remembers a time when some young activists from the National Coordinator of Human Rights followed a directive from their bosses to draft a press release. In their proposal, they equally condemned Shining Path's human rights violations and those of the armed forces. When their bosses, who were all NGO directors and leftist militants, reviewed the draft, they said something like, "We can't place our comrades who went astray on the same level as the military." The young activists insisted on their position, but their bosses never wavered.

It took many years for the Left and so many activists, who are now great democrats, to learn the language and value of democracy. There's no simple way to tell what happened. All we have are imperfect people, failing in moments of crisis, learning in the midst of war—or unlearning old habits, old doctrines.

28   One afternoon some young people told me that a Kantian philosopher, part of the Memory Group, had read a presentation I'd made at the Institute for Peruvian Studies.[5] They said that my comments on Lurgio Gavilán Sánchez's book *Memorias de un soldado desconocido* had given the philosopher a basis to claim in a forum that Gavilán was someone who had justified Shining Path's crimes, who sought exoneration through his testimony, and who wanted to be understood as an instrument who'd been used by others, as an example of the banality of evil. The philosopher described both the book and its author as immoral.

I'm still reflecting on what I wrote back then. Gavilán has a strategy for narrating his life that lets him keep his story moving forward—a terrible story, a story of war, ultimately. That's why he needs to narrate in the first person, but from a child's point of view. That's why the most terrible

---

5. I presented an earlier version of this text in October 2013 in one of the seminars organized by the Memory Group. It circulates on the internet, and other than the terrible writing and spelling mistakes, it's not that different from this one.

events fade into the landscape. That's why he portrays himself as neither guilty of any crimes nor complicit in them. He's a witness.

Academics are stunned by Gavilán, and their critiques of him are surprising for a lot of reasons, at least in part because they're fascinated by the subaltern, by an indigenous person who speaks well, who writes. Gavilán strikes academics as exotic. Those are some limitations of the work and its readers.

But all of this is not the same as labeling Gavilán immoral or flippantly claiming that he wrote his whole book about his life in Sendero and later in the army to justify himself. It's absurd to think that. Gavilán's importance isn't just his story. It's the act itself: that in all his imperfection, he's given us his story, he's exposed his story, exposed himself in it so that we can critique his work and him (the two inevitably get confused), so that we even can pass harsh judgment on him, just as that Kantian philosopher did (unaware of the bitter gift her critique might mean to the one she was accusing), so certain of her truth.

29 Years ago, Hortensia, the leader of an organization for people affected by the violence and an old friend from my early years working in human rights, told me some incredible stories about her father's life. He'd been detained and nearly disappeared in the 1980s, was a migrant in the jungle in the 1990s, and was finally murdered there by the peasant patrols (*rondas campesinas*).

People considered Hortensia part of Shining Path, or somewhat so. She really wasn't. Instead, she was one of those nearly invisible people who, chaotic and confused, help maintain some semblance of order in this cynical and barbaric world. She wanted justice, so she turned her tiny business into a place to support others' causes, helping them despite the precariousness of her own situation. She didn't have the prestige that ANFASEP or other leaders had.

Hortensia didn't do a good job of playing the victim: she wasn't weak, she fought, she argued with the NGOs, she spoke to the military. Her work brought her legal problems and made her a burden for the human rights lawyers.

An army commander, who later became famous for his controversial death, told Hortensia to stop being a nuisance or he'd "take her out." He considered her an ally of the terrorists. This commander made Hortensia walk a long distance into a remote part of the central jungle. Terrified, she felt her final hour had come. They would kill her in a place close to where her father's body had been abandoned. At the end of the journey, in a really inhospitable spot, the commander said to her, "This is it. Here's where the bodies are. Yes, the peasant patrols killed them. And, yes, we collaborated."

When everyone is an accomplice, the term loses meaning. The commander never let go of the idea that Hortensia was a terruca or at least a pawn the terrorists were using. Still, she never stopped feeling fear and gratitude toward him, both at the same time. She remembers how nervous she felt when she ran into him on the street some time later. He embraced her and bought her coffee. He knew—or thought he knew—things about her, but he helped her anyway. He helped his enemy. And those enemies—in reality, members of the MRTA—later killed him . . . perhaps. There are several stories about how he died.

30   We learn certain lessons early in life, civics lessons worth as much as years of schooling. What we felt back then can change, but the basic lesson sticks with us, persistently, because we feel it's true.

Gerardo was a guy from El Agustino, about twenty-five years old, kind of quiet and sweet. He was strong and streetwise but not a brute. Always clean and well shaven, he had short, combed hair parted to one side. He was a tidy guy with a slight smile. He always seemed at peace.

Gerardo and his family came to live in our modest home at the edge of the train tracks. He was always nice to us. He cooked and cleaned and liked things spick-and-span. He didn't talk about politics much; instead, he talked about the simple things in life, his memories, his adventures at school.

After quite some time passed, Gerardo was detained and jailed in the Lurigancho prison.

We visited him a couple of times. He looked the same, always good-natured and attentive, though somewhat skinnier than before. At times he'd leave us by ourselves because he had to carry out tasks for his superiors. He looked more unkempt than usual, not in terms of how he dressed but because he had a couple of days' worth of stubble on his face.

It didn't occur to me then, but now I understand that he must have been tortured by the police. Yet there he was, telling us some amusing anecdotes about the common prisoners.

In late 1985, the Republican Guard brutally thwarted a mutiny that the Shining Path prisoners staged.[6] Around thirty prisoners died. Such mutinies were a strategy that Shining Path used to exert pressure and provoke reactions that they could later capitalize on politically. But the retaliation they sparked in their opponents was always disproportionate; it rattled the people I lived with or knew. They never expected such brutality. Neither did I. We didn't have a television set, but we had a radio and listened to the news. We'd also keep an eye on the newspapers. My mother, Gerardo's wife, and the other prisoners' families spent days protesting desperately outside the prison.

Gerardo died in Lurigancho. We later saw photographs of one of the mutiny's last sites of resistance, the "British pavilion." Forced to stand in front of a wall, various prisoners were bombarded with grenades and flamethrowers. I'm a little unsure now—I have doubts—but the news back then talked about flamethrowers. What stuck with me was seeing the shadows that the oil and gunpowder left on the wall—like negatives of people frozen in the final instant before they ceased to think.

There's a poem that talks about the shadow's mouth. Ever since that day, I haven't stopped thinking about those shadows and their humanity, about the vulgar ways in which human beings can die: pressed against a wall, a mere outline and silhouette, less than an object. That was the lesson.

31 Twenty years later, we ran into Gerardo's wife in one of the attorney general's offices. She was old, gray, tired, trapped in the past, still filing grievances. There was a time when my family hated her a lot because we associated her with my mother's death. But in the corridors of the Public Ministry, she seemed so small and defeated that it moved us. We embraced her.

My sister, always more lucid than the rest of us, said to her softly, "It's time to let this go. Just rest." Momentarily abandoning her hardened way,

---

6. Comisión de la Verdad, *Informe final*, 2:234–236.

Gerardo's wife bent forward and let herself be taken in by the embrace, allowing herself to shed a tear. Then she smiled at us and said, "Get going, *chicos*." "Be on your way, and take care of yourselves," casting us off, as if spinning a web or reciting an incantation.

She's probably still wandering out there, fighting for that man who died thirty years ago, for a shadow on a wall that no longer exists, for someone whom every institution has rejected as a victim, even the human rights organizations. She's as much a ghost as the dead man she mourns.

32   Sometimes Pedro would take me to La Parada market to sell bananas on his food cart. We almost never sold anything, but later I understood that he did this as a facade to coordinate with his Party comrades or talk to leaders from certain areas of the city located in the foothills. In any case, it was interesting for me to experience what it was like to work as a street vendor, to get a feel for the three-wheeled cart and how easy it was to steer it.

Pedro was married to one of my mother's old friends, a small, unkempt, nervous woman, someone who badly wanted to be tough, to rise to the level of the rest of her Shining Path comrades but whose character was weak. At a certain point, both Pedro and his wife wound up living with us. They were like our young *tíos*. All our lives we'd grown accustomed to having tíos, so it wasn't a big deal.

The war provided the backdrop for our family life. This was normal for us, like going to school, fetching water, or going out to play. That's why it didn't seem strange when our house would fill with visitors, almost all of them young and exhausted, carrying packages that we knew contained weapons of different models and sizes.

On several occasions, I'd seen boxes full of tubes wrapped in brown paper, soft to the touch; they felt like big hunks of modeling clay. I was told not to touch them. But one morning, Pedro, perhaps because he thought it was urgent and had no one else to help him, taught me how to work with the synthetic material they used to make dynamite cartridges. It felt like doing shop work in school. You'd flatten the clay and push it into a milk can, add a bit of explosive, and insert a piece of metal, and for a fuse you'd stick some matches on it—or something like that. Most of all, I remember our house flooded with light, all of us kneeling on the ground, talking about everyday things and smelling those interesting materials while, outside, the whole barrio danced around a *yunza* tree. That's why I know it must have been February or March; it was Carnival time, likely 1985.

Back then I didn't give much thought to the morality of what I was doing. What I mean to say is that I didn't think about it at length. But I did know certain things. I wasn't a naive child. If these things were happening in my house, and if my young friends and tíos were doing them with my mother's guidance, then I assumed they had to be on the up-and-up. That's what I believed. My education had been precarious, at least when it came to my schooling, but I was very well read, quite democratic, and very open to dialogue. I was a mature and cultured kid.

When you're taught from childhood to see poverty and be moved by it, it winds up having an effect on you and becomes part of who you are. Saying or writing things like this always sounds pathetic or stupid, especially when you say them publicly, but I don't know any other way to describe it. I'm not sure if every radical leftist family or only some utopian Senderistas practiced such a pedagogy of solidarity and extreme sensitivity, but this was definitely the case for some families. I'm certain, however, that this was how I related to the world. I think that the adult militants in Shining Path, for the most part, saw things similarly. But perhaps because, as a child, I internalized all these feelings and lessons, they became part of my DNA.

So, I'm not sure what my degree of complicity in all of this really is. I helped hide weapons. I burned and transported documents. One summer afternoon I built dynamite cartridges, though I'm not sure what they were going to be used for (but I can presume how they were used).

I did all of this believing in the possibility of a different future. But, at the same time, I hated that life. Little by little I got to observe how miserable Shining Path was and to understand its contradictions—the horrific violence, the fear (fear not for myself but for others, for my family, my father, and later my mother).

And the deaths. So many deaths! The revolution couldn't have had much value if it brought such carnage. Many people already realized that and talked about it. But the ones I knew—I'm not really sure why—didn't get out. They stayed. They stayed.

33 "Are you kidding? No one made a chalkboard?"

It's the winter of 2012. Sara, surprised, glances at the group and affectionately scolds her comrades in the Memory Workshop for being too modern.

"Look," she says patiently, "if we make a chalkboard to announce our event, we can show everyone that we know how to speak to students in their own language. Chalkboards have been our way of communicating important things at this university for decades. It's tradition."

There's no consensus. It seems like a minor issue, but a conflict breaks out. Everyone in the workshop has so little free time. It doesn't seem worth it to spend an evening drawing crooked letters on an old chalkboard when they'll just get washed away by the rain. They try to change Sara's mind.

"Look, Sara, it may be tradition, but the chalkboards are ugly. You can't say they're not. They look like they're from another era, and they're so poorly written."

"Well, that depends on how snazzy we make them look. Our problem is that we're not being creative; it's that we don't know how to do it right. I, however, *do* know how to do it. The rest of you are useless!"

"But what if the chalkboards wind up looking all crazy Marxist?"

"They're not all that way," Sara replies.

"Don't deny it, Sara. The chalkboards around here usually look like Dazibao posters straight out of the Chinese Cultural Revolution."

"No, no, no," she insists. "They're not all like that. Isn't that true, Karen? Tell them that now people make happy-looking chalkboards full of figures and different colors and those silly things that you like so much."

"Oh, so you're saying that giving the design a little flair is silly?"

"I didn't mean to say that," Sara continues. "But these guys don't know anything. All they do is criticize."

"Okay, Sara, but, really, it's obvious that they're ugly."

"What's obvious is that you don't know anything!"

"Yeah, but besides, why would we tire ourselves out making chalkboards if we can just get a banner printed? Simple as that! It's practical. And it's not up for debate! Time marches on: before we had chalkboards; now we have posters. Let's move on to the next agenda item already."

Sara takes a deep breath and sips her tea. She adjusts her glasses and leans forward. "Look," she says in a tired voice, "the students stop to read chalkboards. They actually read them, not like other kinds of publicity. The chalkboards may be crooked and full of misspellings, but even with their shortcomings they're part of our identity. Everyone knows that we use chalkboards to communicate important messages."

They listen to Sara, still indecisive. She finishes with a brutal parting shot: "You guys don't seem like real San Marcos students!"

....

Rewind to 1989 or 1990: a comrade slaps me on the back enthusiastically. He shows me the finished work. I can see how the chalkboard turned out. It has huge red letters on it and a couple of slogans. It's an announcement for a cultural event to honor revolutionary women. In the middle of the chalkboard there's a woman, drawn in red marker on dot-matrix paper, holding her fist in the air, looking toward the horizon, toward victory or the future. I drew her the night before. They called me to the dorms and told me, "You know how to draw, comrade, so support the cause." I had a good time with those kids; they were a bit rough around the edges, but they gave me mandarin oranges and filled me in on the Party's grand plan, its strategic equilibrium, and a bunch of other stuff. I threw my heart into my drawing. I wanted to draw a simple woman, a woman of the people, like any brave woman who works hard and decides to fight for a cause.

I finished the drawing. I was happy with the woman I'd put on paper, beautiful yet strong—perhaps like the women I'm attracted to, without actually realizing it. The point is that I was satisfied with the work.

Maybe that's why I didn't anticipate the barrage of criticism that would suddenly come my way. I felt unanimous rejection. "You've drawn her too feminine. The woman in the picture doesn't reflect our combatants' will. She has to be hardened. But above all, compañero, she has to exude 'class hatred.'" They handed me a marker to correct my error. But something like a confused feeling of freedom of expression and pride stopped me from doing it.

They didn't pressure me. They thanked me for collaborating and said goodbye in a friendly way. But, in reality, I felt their condescension, something like, "What can we expect from this petty bourgeois guy?"

My work hangs on the wall at the university, mutilated. Boorishly, in thick strokes, they've now given the woman a dark look and an angry gesture; they've stripped her of all beauty. They wouldn't allow her to be pretty. She had to be hateful.

I said goodbye. I walked away quietly.

....

Almost twenty-five years later, the kids in the Memory Workshop toil until late on a Thursday night: markers, glue, paper, pencils, jokes, arguments about aesthetics, photographs. True to an age-old tradition, they make progress on creating the biggest chalkboard San Marcos National University has ever seen. And even though, admittedly, it turned out crooked, it's obvious that it has a different kind of spirit. Propped against the wall, welcoming people to the university, gigantic, it seems to indicate, to anyone who knows how to interpret it, that chalkboards, too, harbor their own form of memory—an ugly one!

34   Many years passed. Despite her comrades' protests, my mother forbade us to join Shining Path, as so many other kids in our situation had done. One of my mother's comrades practically recruited me once without asking her. My mother set him straight, threatened him. She told me that she'd gotten involved in this godforsaken war so that we wouldn't have to, so that we could live in peace.

35   But she wasn't sure we'd ever live in peace. She wasn't sure of anything. As time dragged on, she stopped believing in Shining Path. We, her children, got on her case constantly, pointing out the weaknesses and contradictions of her beloved P. We were harsh. We didn't understand back then that it was nearly impossible for her to get out.

Still, today, I only halfway understand her.

But even though she didn't want us to become combatants, she prepared us for life. For years she trained me to resist torture, to hold my breath under water. I could eventually hold it for a long time. She also taught me to control my emotions, never to cry or show weakness, especially when facing my enemies at school. Serenity and resolve were the name of the game.

She told us we should choose a profession with the country's future in mind, that we should think about what the revolution might need in order to sustain it after the war ended. My preference for the humanities made her laugh. "No," she'd tell me. "You should study statistics or physics." She thought I should study something useful so I could help build the new, democratic society.

It's incredible how far from her dreams, from her utopia, we wound up.

36 She walked along the beach. It must have been around midnight. She thought her children would be waiting for her, in vain, to eat sliced hot dogs and French fries—the ones that cost one and a half *soles*—and to talk about politics before they went to bed. That was their routine. She'd like to have told them she wouldn't make it home. But, how could she?

She looked down. She saw the sand, the foam rolling in and out, her feet. She felt the shots, three of them in her back, like pats from a friend who'd been waiting for her for a long time.

She lay down beside the ocean, breathing heavily, thinking about her mother, about how much she missed her mother and her songs and her herbal remedies—still breathing, poorly, poorly, feigning breath, thinking about her children, sudden anguish.

For the first time, she saw blood running into the ocean, abandoning her, leaving her dry, ending her. She breathed again, and then again, however she could. She could hardly breathe.

"I raised them for this." It was as if someone had whispered that thought in her ear, softly. "They'll understand." And then calm washed over her again. And she saw that her blood wasn't abandoning her, that the ocean, calm, embraced it—so that she could live on in the eyes of her descendants.

And she didn't close her eyes, so that she could see them, too. And, at last, she stopped breathing.

37 When my mother died in 1992 and Abimael Guzmán went to jail just a few months later, I suddenly realized that in several ways, my life as I once knew it had ended—and, at the same time, my future.

I'd been educated in values that no longer made sense; they would have mattered only if utopian socialism had become reality. My social skills are worthless now: no more solidarity, no more suffering for others or offering them shelter. But one doesn't shut these things off by pressing a button. The way I spoke was worthless, too: not only was it no longer practical, it was taboo, an object of suspicion. The things I read, my favorite books—all worthless. My friends were dead, my family divided, my siblings separated and confused. But, most of all, I felt like I was alone. I had the strange feeling that I was suddenly the last inhabitant on a planet that no longer existed.

v. Victims

I think we have to move away from being victims.
My son lived for twenty years. He was a poet, too.
And I celebrate those twenty years of life.

Juan Gelman, "Hay que moverse del lugar
de la víctima"

38 Lately, the social sciences and new work on historical memory have insisted on a need to decenter our analyses and move away from the paradigm of human rights.[1] One consequence of this is that the victim ceases to be the main actor in histories of war and in reconstructions of localized memories.[2]

Critiques of a "victim-centered approach" are many and valid. Critics argue that such an approach makes the victim one-dimensional, diverting focus from his or her role as an actor both in wartime and in the postwar era. This approach, too, ignores people's will and motivations and highlights instead only the harm they suffered. It sets in motion

---

1. Currently NGOs, particularly international ones, manage an elaborate framework with concepts such as transitional justice that seek to systematize grave political crises and armed conflicts across the globe, primarily through truth commissions, which they understand as replicable. Gonzáles, "Nuevas fronteras," summarizes this position.

2. See Oglesby, "Educating Citizens"; del Pino and Yezer, *Las formas*.

a purification process that strips actors of their political agency, turning them into innocent victims. It also doesn't help us understand the strategies that communities and individuals use to reflect or not reflect on their memories (i.e., selective memory) or the strategies they deploy when tactically approaching organizations that would defend their rights to political reparations or justice (e.g., NGOs, the state, international organizations). Finally, it doesn't help us analyze the internal dynamics, the micropolitics, that play out in communities such as Ayacucho where everyone is a victim, though some more so than others, and where everyone is a victimizer, though some a little more than others, and where, because of this, the categories of *victim* and *victimizer* don't work.

It's neither unwarranted nor in error that the victim, for decades, was at the center of discourse about the war. But today that urgency has abated. It's not that demands for truth, justice, and reparations have been met. It's that the need to understand the war has also become powerful: the need to understand now has a place alongside the agendas of the victims' organizations and the NGOs.

Every new study reveals the limitations of a victim-centered approach.[3] Towns and neighborhoods are full of memories of people whose experiences were complex, who can't be contained within the categories of victim and perpetrator. In the old victim-centered approach, the war ap-

---

3. Reátegui, *Criterios básicos*, offers a reflection on this perspective on rights, specifically on places of memory. It could be that Reátegui, in an effort to preserve the legacy of the TRC, goes too far in taking from its *Final Report* only what is ethical and responsible to re-present, thus preventing him from understanding current social struggles about local memories (Portugal, *Lugares*). Del Pino and Agüero (*Cada uno*) have underlined this. But is Reátegui completely wrong? Perhaps motivated by our search to find different voices and to criticize transitional justice, we overlook something important that Reátegui insists on: If we don't commemorate the victims, then why commemorate? And the answer is: we remember not just to commemorate, and we commemorate for others besides the victims. The victims themselves are destabilized as a point of reference, and thus we also need to ask: (a) What is the point of reference for a politics of memory? (b) If we commemorated radically and not as part of a negotiation that allows commemoration, wouldn't that be sufficient to add purpose to the memorial? (c) Even if a memorial site doesn't have any more impact than simply being there, has it necessarily failed as a visible object? What would it mean for it to be successful? What would it need to prompt among citizens? It's true, to remember and to honor might not be enough, but in this indifferent and cynical society, is that so little? Isn't a little bit of respect radical?

pears extraordinary, like a break in the history of communities or neighborhoods. It's as if the war befell them, as if they had little to do with it, as if their only connection to the war were suffering. Nor is the experience of the state, at least of the armed forces, a simple memory of evil.

We need subjects with agency, people with will, motivations, and political profiles. We don't need any more victims, people caught in the crossfire—no more miserable innocents.

39 But before we recover the actor and cast aside the victim with such academic zeal, it might be important to think about a few things.

We might want to think about the forces that shaped, conditioned, and influenced people's decisions, or that made it difficult if not impossible for them to make those decisions, or that plunged them into the dilemma of having to make decisions whose costs—moral, economic, political, or simply human—were extreme. We're already familiar with some of those costs: having to decide to kill neighbors, family members, or Shining Path militants to prove their loyalty to the armed forces.

In many cases, that was agency—a miserable kind of agency.

40 Elizabeth Jelin, critiquing the prevalence of the human rights paradigm, claims that if we preserve the victim's cultural centrality, then the things a person did no longer matter; all that matters is what was done to that person.[4] A victim-centered approach eclipses the actor and instead foregrounds a defenseless, depoliticized individual; it emphasizes only that people's rights were violated and that they suffered. If we reassess the actor, we take a step toward restoring his or her complex humanity.[5]

But how can we recover the actor? How deep should we go? Which actors should we recover? And who should recover them? I think these questions are still quite superficial.

Isn't it enough to recover people's suffering, which is already a lot to take on, so that they can be acknowledged in the way they deserve? No, it's not.

---

4. Jelin, *Los trabajos de la memoria*, 71–72.

5. Torres, interview.

We have to recover and expose the entirety of their miserable lives—every bit of their small, ruinous, simple, miserable lives, so that we academics can understand certain processes better and write about them, or, if we have ethical motivations, so that society can take a better look at itself and learn civic lessons.

Yet, when has taking a close look at the actors in a war or a massacre made us better? Does knowing that a carpenter felt hatred at dawn and in the afternoon went out to buy bread somehow prepare us to confront the days he didn't live to see, the days following his torture?

Is it more valuable to focus on what people did than on what was done to them? Doesn't what was done to them, what their bodies endured, tell us more about the type of life and death that fate destined them to share with others of their time and generation? Isn't what was done to them part—perhaps the most vital part—of how their bodies resisted, faded away, and let themselves be molded? Can we not find an archaeology of the mechanisms of violence written on their bodies, like a trace?

It pains me not to understand—not to be sure of these things, not to be able to let go of pain enthusiastically as a bad anchoring point, let go of tragedy as an error, and instead look at violence with the purpose of embracing a whole life. "By all the delights that I shall miss, / Help me to die, O Lord." William Hodgson wrote these words two days before he died in one of the most horrible battles of the last century.[6] Fear was his agency. He wanted and asked for help so he could be a soldier, so he could be a man, so he could have an ending to his story.

Fear . . . Fear . . . We have to recover not only the terror one feels when confronting danger but also the fear that destroys all certainty, the fear that a small, exposed, and confused person feels when facing horror. Might feeling a little bit of that fear calm our enthusiasm?

41 "We waited for them at night. We let them in, just like always, telling them their food was there. They arrived suspecting nothing. Once inside, we took them by surprise and tied them up. Only one of them had

---

6. William Noel Hodgson (1877–1918) was a British author who wrote in multiple genres. He was killed in World War I, hit by an artillery shell in the Fourth Battle of Ypres. The poem is titled "Before Action" (1916).

a weapon. We all dragged them out to the plaza, beating them, stoning them, clubbing them. Then we killed them with machetes. They were just boys. Two of them were schoolkids from this very place. We buried them in a nearby field and kept it a secret. The next year, members of that organization took their revenge on us for rebelling against them. They killed almost all our leaders."

The members of one community told me a story like this. But they didn't tell just me; everyone who has dealt with these matters has heard not only dozens but hundreds of similar stories, stories of victims' families. We've heard about victims chopped into pieces by Shining Path or by the military in front of their children, spouses, or parents. And I'm talking about victims who were killers, too, doing "micropolitics."

Desperation and fear are, therefore, part of the agency we need to recover. That's fine. But we have to do it unselectively and without compromise. We have to call things by their name and assume the consequences.

In a presentation at LUM, Ponciano del Pino urged us to pay attention to the "impurities of war" in order to narrate the war's complexity.[7] I understand what he's trying to say. I even share his motivation: to move beyond naive, stereotypical narratives. But I also think that we have to set aside this kind of rhetoric because, when we use it, we delude ourselves all the more: just as language seems to tell us something, it also masks our confusion. There are no purities or impurities in war. Horror is just that—horror! We have to recover it, describe it, relive it, and later flesh out its consequences. We have to look at ourselves without trickery, examine our shared or individual filth, and see if we can recognize ourselves in it.

---

7. Ponciano del Pino, remarks at book presentation of del Pino and Yezer, *Las formas* (LUM, June 5, 2014). With the term *impurezas*, del Pino alludes to Primo Levi's well-known gray zone, which in Peru was rediscovered by those who want to argue that there weren't victims "caught in the crossfire" and that not everything can be reduced to innocent victims and perpetrators. However, it is worth asking whether there weren't actually victims caught in the crossfire. It is necessary to revisit this question without naivete and the pressure to defend, which was the mandate of the time when these narratives were constructed. Can we really believe that because they had a small margin of action these peasant communities weren't caught in a crossfire that ultimately engulfed them? It's not a matter of pitting one myth against another. This needs to be studied in detail.

42   Another nonexistent victim.

"They electrocuted me, waterboarded me, all those things you already know. Later, those bastards raped me. For days, weeks, I lost track of time. But I didn't break the golden rule. I didn't give them any information. I don't know if I was alone or if someone else was there. But someone was there; I could hear slow breathing. But I was blindfolded. I couldn't tell if it was another detained woman or someone from DIRCOTE. I thought I would die there. But, you see, they took me to prison. I got sick, and now this is how I am [she walks with difficulty], because of the torture. But who cares? Here, no one knows any of this. If they did, what would I do? They'd fire me on the spot from my job at the school."

This Shining Path woman participated actively in missions in Lima. She killed. She irreparably harmed dozens of families. But she's not crazy, nor is she a sadistic monster. She's not helpless either, as we typically classify human rights victims. She's a woman from the city who was born in a marginal and dangerous neighborhood. But for a variety of reasons—whether generational or familial, or because of her own inclinations, or because of influences on her, or because of a thousand other things—she joined Shining Path. We found ourselves there, facing a woman who had committed crimes but whose motivations were not—how shall I say it—base.

I asked my mother if they tortured her when they detained her, prior to her imprisonment in the Chorrillos Prison. She never shared any details. She'd always say, "Later." That's because she never felt like a victim, nor did she want us to think of her that way; she also managed sensitive information as anyone would around his or her loved ones: to protect them. But I can assume that she was tortured—and that they also could have raped her, as they did with this old woman who spoke to me from behind a wooden table draped in a checkered, plastic tablecloth.[8]

---

8. My brother once again correctly points out that when we were little, we didn't grow up with the anguish of thinking that our mother could be raped—tortured, yes, but not raped. Yet the way I wrote this makes it appear that this fear was part of our anguish. It's true that we didn't live with this fear, but now I know that it could have happened, that our mother could have been raped. Memory is not the only resource on this topic. The TRC confirmed that the vast majority of women prisoners they interviewed had suffered sexual violence by the security forces. And although my memory doesn't include this fear, looking back from the present, I see that I should have feared it. It's a revelation to perceive the fears that ignorance or childhood masks. But today I want to tell it this way because these women—the survivors, those *terrorists*—have rights.

These terrorists or former terrorists—these guilty women—didn't want to be victims. Nor has anyone bothered to construct them as such. To say "terruco" or "terruca" is like saying "witch" or "devil." It's a label that brands a person as horrible, a mistake, a dreadful person, a foreigner to the community, someone who needs to be eliminated. When one is entrenched in such language, it's impossible to recover who those individuals were as political subjects.

When we dismantle the centrality and social function of victimhood, are we really thinking seriously about people like these, who haven't even had the pitiful consolation of being treated as victims by their communities? If we're correct about needing to move beyond the idea of the victim, in what nameless wasteland will these people wind up, in what nameless place within our world of memories and rights?

They are ghosts who can't even be victims, because they are unnameable in conventional language. They're semisubjects.

43 I've known him since I was a teenager. He sold books at the university. When everyone was being detained or killed, he disappeared. I didn't think much about him. Later, I saw him again, alive. The first time that we casually bumped into one another he avoided my eye contact, which was my way of gesturing to greet him. He still avoids me. Each of us knows that the other knows, and that must make him uncomfortable.

What place does this old Shining Path militant have in this story, this man who isn't just guilty but who's also "traitor"? Did our world full of normal citizens vindicate him simply because, at the time, possibly pressed by torture, he gave up his former comrades and collaborated with state security agents? What does that make him?

This poor guy whom my mother fed so many times—who suffered so much, and whom I remember as a happy, somewhat foolish kid—I wish he wouldn't avoid me and that he'd talk to me knowing that he has nothing to hide, that no one can blame anyone for how they managed to survive the horror.

That's his agency, and that's what I'm trying to recover. It's OK to do it. We need to go through this hard, critical, even cruel exercise—because truth isn't an absolute, nor is it just a word (or maybe it is, I don't know); perhaps it's a gradual process of revealing, with effort and patience, some ultimate meaning that, at present, we can barely sense. So, if this is correct, then we also have to think about what truth is and how much stock we're willing to put in it.

44   That's why when we write and strive to decentralize victimhood and think instead about the many subjective experiences that wars create, we have to remember that there are many memories. Constructing victims isn't just a discursive move. Victims get constructed even before (or at the same time as) bodies and the human will suffer coercion. Victims are born when people are destroyed. Victimhood alludes to a process, however ephemeral, in which an individual or a community is subjected to someone else's will, which in turn impedes the individual's or the community's reproduction.[9]

Victimhood is like a brand. It doesn't get erased simply with the passage of time or because the social sciences need to understand societies and their conflicts better. The day before a man is tortured he's many things: a worker, a father, a union leader, a soccer player. The day after he survives torture he's a wounded man, a prisoner, a suspect, a guilty party, a potential disappeared person, or a hero. But all of these new properties become part of him only when he's labeled a victim. And how long will they remain part of him?

Who decides? And who decides when a person will no longer be a victim?

45   To be a victim is unstable. There are people who want to be labeled victims. They'll pursue that brand because it gives meaning and respect to a life that was once only death, just another cadaver. Victimhood gives people a status they desire, and they perceive that this is just. In that sense, to be a victim is a trophy, an honor, a form of dignity.

---

9. I would like to underline this basic point: Nobody wants to be a victim of horror. It's not just a matter of language or the discourse of those involved; it's an expression of their bodies. And here I want to develop the argument made by Manrique, "Generando"; del Pino and Yezer, *Las formas*; del Pino and Agüero, *Cada uno*; and a separate international literature, intrigued with the rediscovery that victims are also people.

46   Time also matters. Victimhood remains on the horizon of younger generations, as in Spain's transition to democracy. After all the political pacts, the forgotten dead, and the hidden mass graves—the price Spain paid for stability—the dead eventually were rescued, their victimhood restored to them. What I mean to say is that, in this case, the term *victim* doesn't take anything away but rather adds something; it makes it so that deaths that happened in the past now become public knowledge, so that society can finally name what happened. The status of *victim* completes the description.

47   We should also critique and approach suspiciously the iconoclastic zeal to destroy labels such as *victim* and *innocent*. If there are no victims, then we're all the same; no one is guilty. History explains everything. Responsibilities become nothing more than a matter of individual morality and relativism, unnecessary for understanding the past and political life.

Social processes, contexts, and medium- and long-term causes eclipse human will. And when human intention falls out of play, other things fall away, too, such as assigning guilt and the need for remedies (both personal and collective) for the harm done to human actors.

48   To be a victim is a long, complex process that we can discuss and historicize because, more than anything, it's an accumulation of losses. The victim has suffered, and this suffering has its history, its milestones, its contradictions, its moments of decision, its rhythms, its crises.

People are deprived of all they can be and could have been. This drastic change in a life's possibilities is the victim's essential condition: his or her life has been disrupted in the extreme. Daily life stops. What would naturally come the next day is forestalled. This change affects the most ordinary and, at the same time, the most intimate aspects of life.

Remember, eternally remember
all the unknown dead of Hiroshima:
the old fisherman who had woven
with strands of sun a new net
through which
petals of the ocean shone

like perfumed violets;
the man who fell in front of his house
at the precise instant at which smiling toward his children
he showed them
an old bicycle he'd just bought
. . .
the girl who in fifteen minutes
was supposed to meet her boyfriend. . . .[10]

Eugen Jebeleanu wrote these words, paralyzed by how a few seconds of future could suddenly be cut off, as if they had never been part of a time sequence that would have made them (almost) inevitable and logical.

The victims' experience belongs to them and their families; the families are another kind of victim. Yet it's not only up to them to understand and analyze that experience. This is true. But understanding cannot—if it's to be complete—fail to consider the victims' condition and their real existence. To understand is not simply to think about victimhood as a label or a strategy for defending human rights.

Because in war, harm is a key to understanding human relations. Harm founds the victims' world. Communities are full of victims. That's the first thing we have to remember when we approach them. The country, the whole world, is a mass grave. If we're not honest with ourselves about that, we fall into intellectual arrogance, snobbery, or, even worse, a new vice that characterizes human rights institutions, and that's equally as bad as the narcissistic activism we've seen in the past: technocracy.

49   In countries such as Peru that have suffered war, long years of silence, dictatorship, and a truth commission—and that have promoted both a handful of trials and the gradual bureaucratization of justice and reparations, which in the long run have become unstoppable—intellectuals get somewhat anxious.

In workshops and at conferences, we tend to hear things like, "The truth commission's report is just a catalog of what happened" or "We have to deepen our understanding of memory." And although these

---

10. Jebeleanu, "Canto a los muertos," 24.

statements seem reasonable to me, it's as if they are two or three decades behind the times. Many victims have moved on to other concerns, have died, or are very old. But we still have to rescue them from oblivion or stagnation.

There's a short story by Isaac Asimov: the one about the alien monkeys who watch and wait for the earthlings to kill one another so they can take over with their science, decontaminate everything, rescue the survivors, and create a new society. The alien monkeys are convinced that theirs is the most benevolent race in the universe. But the earthling, a regular guy whom the monkeys capture to analyze, tells the aliens that "they're vultures."[11]

Seated tonight in the auditorium at the Pontifical Catholic University of Peru, listening to the experts on transitional justice speak so passionately, I realize that I share certain technical knowledge with them, even though deep down that expertise strikes me as debased: a whole discipline of experts standing untarnished as they scrutinize the people who have killed each other in excess.

50 Neville Chamberlain became a marked man in twentieth-century history, perhaps unjustly: he's remembered as the sad mediator. He didn't gain anything from the concessions he made to Hitler, not even much time. He simply gave the Nazis the proof they needed of their coercive skills and of their main rival's weakness.

I think about the TRC, the NGOs, and the Reparations Council.[12] Without taking anything away from them, they've achieved a lot over the years, even considering their limitations. But their defensive position—making concessions to the powers that be in the spirit of realpolitik so as to secure some benefit for those affected by the violence—has also had medium- and long-term costs.

The Reparations Council, the institution that most embodied the TRC's work in its aftermath, exemplifies the perpetual tension that arises

---

11. Asimov, "Gentle Vultures."

12. The Consejo de Reparaciones (the Reparations Council), part of the Justice Ministry, creates the list of those eligible for individual and collective reparations from the Peruvian state.

in world history from making concessions. The council has suffered mistreatment, sudden budgetary and personnel cuts, temporary closures, leadership changes, media trashing, and complaints. And this has been going on for years! Yet it has endured. It has tolerated everything. The question is: Couldn't the people on the council have simply screamed, "Enough!"? Couldn't they have chosen to reject the blatant hostility, to reject how various governments have shunned reparations? Perhaps if they had done this, the process we currently have for documenting victims would have been thwarted. But perhaps we would have gained ground in recovering other meanings of the past.

It has generally become accepted that victims linked to Shining Path shouldn't receive reparations. These victims know full well that one of their nonnegotiable human rights has been negotiated away. I know a lot of people—and assuredly the council knows many more—who were labeled terrorists and who, because of this, and without ever having been legally judged as such, have been left off the list of victims. We can't look at these people as more of a victim or as more innocent than anyone else (if we want to use that terminology), as more innocent than I or many others who roll through life peacefully.

I remember when the leader of a group of displaced people was told that he could no longer serve as a leader in his home region of Apurímac. He was an organizer, the heart and soul of that small base of activism. But he was never going to be listed as a victim on the official registry.[13] He was always smiling, and still is. He accepted all of it. He understood. But I'm sure he felt alone, confused.

51   The reasons that motivate some researchers to do away with a victim-centric perspective strike me as useful. We have to decenter the victim, to show that peasants were, in fact, politicized and that they'd

---

13. The Registro Único de Víctimas (Sole Register of Victims), overseen by the Reparations Council, and the Comisión Multisectorial de Alto Nivel (High-Level Multisector Commission) are the two entities in charge of implementing the individual and collective reparations established by the Peruvian state for those affected by the violence. As of 2015, more than 180,000 people were on the council's list of those eligible for reparations. Nevertheless, reparations have been in many ways a failure, a lack of respect toward the victims and their families.

done politics in their own way for a long time. People remember anecdotes about Uchuraccay, about how peasants played their part as "poor" and premodern, and then, a minute later, as soon as the meeting with the truth commissioners had ended, they'd ask everyone to photograph the occasion.

I bring this up to call attention to something. Deconstructing the victim should take a back seat to another pressing need: the need to fight against Lima-centric and racist explanations. A research (and political) agenda that decenters the victim is welcome. But should we carry out that agenda at the expense of diminishing or disappearing another problem that resulted from the war? Should rescuing peasants from their subordinate role in history mean that other victims disappear?

52 A strong push against victim-centrism has taken root among memory scholars. It's not unwarranted. Victims don't ask to be treated as such: they don't want people to treat them as if they had some kind of disability. They stress this more and more. Instead, they want to be recognized as fighters, leaders, people who aren't paralyzed by tears. They don't want others to see them as weeping Blessed Virgins.

It's interesting that researchers and those affected by the violence agree on this issue, because the two groups tend not to listen to one another. Researchers often find support when they iconoclastically thwart the rhetoric of human rights movements, either enthusiastically or cynically (depending on the researcher). Not long ago, I heard someone at LUM say that testimony can show us only victims and that truth commissions, by their nature, can construct only innocent victims; this situation limits our ability to see the complexities of violence. Someone at LUM also said that those who testified to the TRC were more interested in being seen as victims than as "owners of a truth," which is how one might assume they should understand themselves. Seen in this way, the commission could only aspire to limit the field of possible lies people tell about the past.[14]

14. Ludwig Huber, remarks at book presentation of del Pino and Yezer, *Las formas* (LUM, June 5, 2014). Yet I want to ask: Can those affected by violence access a truth commission in any capacity other than as victims? Can they do it as responsible citizens fulfilling their duty to reconstruct historical memory for the good of the community? Why

There are so many more interesting, revealing, and challenging things that we can still say about this subject. It's worth staying alert and being critical of ourselves.

Is it true that a testimonial account can produce only a victim? And if this is true, is it necessarily bad? Is it counterintuitive to think that testimony can produce something other than a victim? Doesn't the affected person's need to be heard take precedence? Doesn't the offense take precedence? When a violent offense marks someone's life, he or she can react in many ways: keep silent, take revenge, speak out hoping to achieve personal catharsis, denounce what happened, express confusion, or all of these things at once or at different times. Testimony is just one way of sharing experience. And when we're talking about horrible experiences, then perhaps the one who speaks *is* a victim: a real victim who's been lucky enough to be heard. Testimony isn't mere wordplay.

Testimony doesn't exhaust experience. It underlines, if you will, a painful moment and adds another dimension to a fluid identity. Whether we call someone a victim or something else is a matter of convention.

53   A while after my father was killed on El Frontón Island, perhaps a year later, we were organizing our clothes in burlap sacks that we used as closets. And maybe because we were talking about my father, much to my surprise, I cried. I didn't know then, nor do I know now, if I was crying over him. I cried for but a moment, silently, without attaching my pain directly to his death or his absence. My mother, moved, accompanied me in my brief seconds of weakness. Later, she told me I shouldn't cry, that the best way to honor my father was by not abandoning the ideals for which he fought. But she had tears in her eyes, too. They lasted but an instant. She'd taught us not to show our feelings.

"I understand," I assented, nodding my head, not saying another word. Silently, we kept organizing our clothes for just a little while longer.

Even today I don't cry about my father or my mother. I don't visit them on important anniversaries. I don't go to the Nueva Esperanza cemetery

....

should we ask that they present themselves in ways that we don't expect of ourselves? If a member of our own family disappeared, wouldn't we go to the commission to talk about them and our pain?

where my mother is buried or to the island where some bit of my father must remain. I've resisted being a victim. I don't want people to pity me. I've also suspected that people wouldn't be very empathetic to my experience anyway. The son of terrorists, no matter how wrong his parents' deaths may have been, has to be at least a little bit evil.

But even if I don't want to be a victim, does that mean that others don't need to be seen that way? Aren't there people out there longing for their pain to be validated, so it's worth something? Is it so hard to create space for them within our typology of those devastated by war?

54 Victimization is the victimizers' problem. It's especially a problem for those who act as intermediaries between those who have suffered harm and the public and academic spheres, that is, for those who mediate access to rights, prestige, or even solace.

The victims remain there—independently of who is doing the victimizing—even if people erase them from speech or refuse to see them. In some corner of the world, secretly, someone pities a family member who has suffered in war. Perhaps the one feeling pity is your neighbor. And you may never know it because that neighbor has kept quiet about it his or her whole life.

55 Therefore, victimization is sometimes a political strategy that gives access to justice and other scarce resources. Those who suffer human rights violations learn this. They adapt to it. They appropriate the tools and language of international law and leverage them to their benefit. How is that surprising? Are we surprised that they behave as any of us would? Are we surprised that they show their wounds to get a little attention? Should this surprise us if we remember that before they became victims society had already excluded them?

This strategy makes sense. It has a purpose. It's reasonable. Still, in acknowledging the value in their approach, it's impossible not to ask if there isn't something lost when certain communities strategically leverage suffering—something of the ethical power of a complaint made with no aspiration other than its own justice.

But it's not our place to judge others so severely without judging ourselves, at least a little.

56   I want to say this: in countries such as ours where it's so hard to have any kind of status, being a victim is at least something, perhaps a step toward citizenship.

As we launch our critiques, I simply ask that we think about this a little, about how delicate it can be to take that step.

57   I remember how I felt when I crossed paths at the morgue with a longtime leader of a victims' organization. She and I were supposedly there to receive my father's remains. It was offensive, a farce, but we went there to see, anyway.

She saw me near the exit and approached me, frenetic and nervous. She gave me a hug and cried. She said, "Josecito, you've spent many years helping us and, secretly, you had your own worries." We walked across the street, and I bought her an herbal tea. I felt strange. As we left, she insisted on consoling me: "All these years you were one of us."

I sensed underlying joy in her words: a warm feeling, as if someone shared her plight, as if I were even more on her side.

But I left confused. The fact that some members of the victims' organization knew my secret might take something away from the years of work I did out of a sense of honor and solidarity—never as an extension of my own needs. I had worked in solidarity with the victims because their stories touched me and because I believed their struggles were just. But what if all the work I did had been only to help myself?

My dear friend—where might she be? When she embraced me and counted me among her inner circle, I thought, "No, I'm not the same as you. I'm not a victim. What happened to me was part of some other process. It's a brutal fact but not the basis of my identity." But maybe, just maybe I rejected her only because I wasn't ready to surrender, to set aside my pride, as my mother had done years earlier in another context.

VI. The Surrendered

> Do I walk? Have I feet still? I raise my eyes, I let them move round, and turn myself with them, one circle, one circle, and I stand in the midst. All is as usual. Only the Militiaman Stanislaus Katczinsky has died. Then I know nothing more.
>
> **Erich Maria Remarque**, *All Quiet on the Western Front*

58   I am the son of Shining Path militants who died in Lima in the mid-1980s and early 1990s. They were killed extrajudicially. I never protested for them. My family and I didn't stake our identity on loss, the damage we suffered, or the search for justice and reparations. Yes, I've been searching for a long time for a legitimate place from which to write, speak, and act in public space. It hasn't been, nor is it, easy.

Like others, I've asked myself for a long time if guilt can be inherited, transformed into shame about one's origins or ancestors. If society and the state don't consider me a legitimate victim, can I claim any consolation? And do I have the right to forgive someone?

Forgiveness is a gift. In that sense, only certain people and groups that belong to an indulgent economy can grant it. To forgive, I must first be a victim. And, symbolically, to be a victim is a positive thing; it has lots of positive connotations (even though, paradoxically, victimhood is founded on suffering).

In theory, the son of dead terrorists doesn't have the positive qualities needed to give him social and symbolic capital.

At a time when academics around the world are seeking to decenter the victim from their analyses and from politics, I want to point out that, in some cases, we need the opposite: to throw caution to the wind and create a climate of acceptance in which people can be seen as victims. We have to accept the cost of doing this and make ourselves vulnerable, knowing that it's only as victims that certain people can have a voice and a past.

I need to recover my past without turning Shining Path into a myth, without humanizing it. I need to reconstruct Shining Path's complex experience without caving to the pressure of the powers that be and feeding into their lies. The powers that be don't always represent democracy's triumph; it's not that simple.

I understand that some people try not to think in victim-centric terms. I'm suggesting the opposite: that I become a victim for the first time so I can have the opportunity to forgive and, later, to surrender, that is, to stop being a victim and hand myself over completely to the judgment, scrutiny, and compassion of others.

59   Stig Dagerman wrote that we have an insatiable need for consolation.[1] This makes me think of an imprisoned woman from the MRTA, whom filmmaker Martha Dietrich once told me about in an intense conversation. The woman had suffered torture. She was incredibly damaged and forever altered, but she still struggles, feebly, to go on living. Doesn't she deserve consoling? Does it make someone feel good to see her there, at her breaking point, in the name of some imperfect idea of justice?

I think about our soldiers, our military—not just about the officials but about the common troops that Mariano Aronés has talked about in his work.[2] Yes, they killed and died, and now, abandoned by their institutions, they suffer the consequences of having accepted the responsibility to fight against Shining Path. Of course, they deserve reparations—but is that all they deserve? Are they entitled only to a formulaic remedy

---

1. Dagerman, *Nuestra necesidad*.
2. Aronés, "Si no matas, te matan."

that, in the end, is just a political tactic? Don't they deserve acceptance and thanks?

I think about Fujimori, my close lawyer friends, and the organizations of victims and their families that have been so vital to the struggle against impunity. I wonder if everyone engaged in that fight hasn't crossed a line in their demands for "total forgiveness" or "neither forgetting nor forgiveness"—or in their implacable criticism of Fujimori's sham attempts to peddle forgiveness. In their opinion, that vile man's attempts don't rise to the level of authentic forgiveness. Should we expect them to? Where does forgiveness start? Primo Levi said that there was no such thing as generalized forgiveness: one can't forgive a group or a country or "the Germans," but one can forgive those who repent, not just with words but with actions that say that they're no longer the people they once were.

Levi knew that justice isn't a small thing and that, really, it's the exception in life; it's just that we don't recognize how exceptional it is because we all take part in the theatrics of our communities and institutions. Forgiveness can't be a novelty, a pretext, or an easy rhetorical strategy for those who'd like to turn the page on the past. In Levi's estimation, he had to keep fighting against those who continued to cause harm and sided with his enemies.[3] But doesn't that keep us somehow tethered to the will of the unjust? Should we trade our ability to forgive because some people stubbornly insist on hatred?

60   I felt this way for the first time when I was working for a human rights organization and we won a very important case for Peru in the Inter-American Court of Human Rights. We had intense discussions with the leader of the Victims' Relatives Organization. He didn't want to value what we'd achieved. He wanted to destroy everyone: those who humiliated him in the Pardons Commission, the NGO workers who denied him support, those who stigmatized him. But what most distanced me from him was his insatiable desire to expose other victims related to the case, whom he suspected were opportunists or possible informants for state agents. His idea of justice struck me as extreme, as justice without

---

3. Levi, *La trilogía*.

mercy. It seemed unnecessary to involve those other victims because they had been overtaken by forces beyond their control. They had already suffered so much, for many years, and they were victims, just like him. And if his suspicions were correct, their Calvary had already been paved with guilt, with the fallout of their betrayal. Not all justice has to happen in court.

I've felt this way on other occasions, too, when I've seen the belligerent attitudes friends and comrades adopt toward their political rivals. At times, they seem overcome by an impulse toward open confrontation, toward outbursts that draw a line in the sand between angels and demons. They take a Manichaean view of the state and its functionaries. In their minds, the state and its agents are nothing but tricksters. They almost seem to hope that everything will end in a bloodbath just to confirm their theory that the state is repressive.

I also take issue with how they treat the police—as if the police were objects to be kicked, insulted, and denigrated, "dirty cops" turned into the butt of propaganda, caricatures, or clever street graffiti. In my life, I've worked a bit with the police, and I know they're not saints. But I understand that they—at least the ones I know—can also experience fear and that they'd prefer to be more than mere cannon fodder with which to wound or by which to be wounded. It doesn't matter to some people what these "cops" are like in real life. All that matters to them is that the cops get labeled and turned into dehumanized enemies.

It's true that Fujimorista politicians and leaders, or those in MOVADEF, are not just political enemies; more accurately, they might be enemies of democracy and, for that reason, they deserve harsher treatment and more careful and stalwart vigilance. But even here, we need to learn more about them, to make a serious and honest effort to understand them—not just vilify and belittle those who make certain choices, who aren't leaders, or who, for different reasons, support certain choices or, minimally, fail to reject them. There are many people who fall into this category.

I'm not sure if others feel the same way, but I've never liked slogans such as "Never forget, never forgive," so sure of themselves, of what's right— or "Forgetting is full of memory," so naively vacuous in its appeal to the simple idea that the past heals us and that memory has many facets. Nor do I like other slogans we've inherited from the past, such as "The people's blood will never be forgotten."

So much blood never will be forgotten! It lives with us. We remember it, rhetorically, every time we walk through Lima. And what does it evoke? Does it remind us that our community is built on a river of blood on which we all float?

I agree that the bloodshed will not be forgotten. How can tens of thousands of crimes be forgotten within a couple of generations (or even longer, as we've learned from Europe, China, or Korea)? Indeed, these crimes are not forgotten. But even if that's true, does it necessarily mean that we automatically need to make denouncing them our life's work and activist mission? I'm not so sure.

How do so many "democratic" friends manage to float above all of the scum and blood? From what pristine pedestal do they ask us not to forget, not to forgive, not to reconcile?

How can I keep from speculating about others who have more merits than I? I stand with the victims' families and participate in their organization's activities because it's crucial to demand justice when faced with impunity. But the message we communicate—our most fundamental message—saddens me. I'm not talking about our message that affirms our right to air our grievances and demand that the guilty be persecuted and punished. I'm disconcerted by our savage messaging about our political culture. So, I accompany the families silently.

Can there be too much justice? Is it like too much love or too much hate? These days, my friends' rabid pursuit of justice at all costs makes me take distance from them. Their lust for justice diminishes its restorative and creative potential and bolsters instead its power to condemn, sanction, prohibit, and repress. I don't know.

I'm pained by all the mockery and ridicule about Fujimori's health, the jokes about his cancer and his body, the violation of his privacy, the humiliation of his family, and the slogans and caricatures about his tongue covered in sores.

Obviously the Fujimoris of the world don't deserve credit, and Fujimori's medical charts have likely been altered to gain sympathy or possible amnesty. The Fujimoristas have a penchant for systematic lies. Their political group and media allies behave cynically and unscrupulously. It's therefore worthwhile and imperative that we resist their attacks.

Pinochet's comic drama, the mortifying farce he staged when he returned from London to Santiago, is still fresh in so many people's minds. Fujimori shouldn't be pardoned; he does not deserve pardon under our laws. He also shouldn't receive treatment that's any different from the treatment any other Peruvian would receive in a similar situation: those rotting away in the horrible jails that the Ministry of Justice oversees. For what it's worth, everyone should be evaluated with equal care. But that's not my point.

This is just a personal feeling, but I wouldn't want to build my militancy in the human rights movement on a foundation of cruelty or irresponsibility. I don't take comfort in degrading anyone, not even the worst criminal. I don't get excited about marching so that a sick man can be kept in jail. I have a hard time sharing the satisfaction of those who are so sure of their moral superiority.

I know that justice can't be bought on a street corner. We have to nurture it, all the more in a country where we have so little of it. Alberto Fujimori has to pay for his crimes and should do it in prison. But should we have to pay for his crimes, too, by making the law a burden, a language devoid of compassion?

61 I think about the marines who killed my father. Early on, Shining Path gathered precise data not only about the marine officials who led the operation but also about those who tortured and killed my father with their own hands. We received detailed information relatively soon after my father was killed. "Here it is. We did our job," was the Party's message.

I think that when Shining Path shared this information with us, they did so not just because the Party was acting responsibly toward its ranks; they also did it to plant in us the seeds of hatred and vengeance, to serve the target up to us on a silver platter.

The same thing happened when my mother was killed. First, a couple of state security agents invited me to drive around Lima and told me that they'd be trailing me at the university and that I should watch my back. I was ultimately thankful for their threats, because I didn't die. Later, a messenger from Shining Path met me several times at the School of Social Sciences and invited me to take my parents' place and avenge their deaths, calling them heroes of the revolution. He told me that they'd identified the three guys who killed my mother.

The guy from Sendero made me sick, with his cheap manipulation strategy. He didn't even give me a couple of weeks to grieve. I sent him packing. And I threatened him, too. I told him that I had my own contacts within the Party—that I knew a lot of people and that I'd do some digging because I wasn't exactly certain who had killed my mother. He was furious. He forbade me to have any contact with the Party other than him. But Shining Path ultimately left me alone.

I never thought about revenge. If justice is compelled to pursue the guilty, then go ahead; that's honorable, even for the guilty.

If a powerless, illegitimate voice like mine matters, I'd prefer that those people who may have killed my parents remain anonymous. Perhaps the passage of time has led them to reflect on what they did, though we can't be sure that it has, nor can we expect it. That can't be my reason for holding onto them; it's not enough. I'm not sure if my reasoning is sound, but, for now, I don't want their children to inherit any stigma. I want to give those men an opportunity to leave their children the best versions of themselves.

62 I think about Alan García, who we know was directly responsible, along with his political leaders, for the deaths of the prisoners at El Frontón, Lurigancho, and Santa Bárbara. We don't need legal verdicts to know that. Truth doesn't materialize on sheets of paper. I also think about the negligent and contemptuous decisions García made during his second term that led to the deaths of workers, police officers, and people who were protesting to gain but a scrap of citizenship.

Should I hate Alan García the same way that my grandmother did, that my mother did? I prefer to forgive him, too. Let him defend himself where and how he can. If the judiciary deems him responsible, then let him face the consequences. But I think he was also overcome by his fears and limitations, that the war was too much for him, that he lost his soul along the way. And when a man loses his soul, we all, in a way, lose it with him. In the face of such destruction, even if I wanted to, I couldn't wish anything worse on him. And so, I find myself wanting to commiserate with him. But how?

The enemies, the guilty: that's what my parents were. And so were those politicians. And so were the soldiers who killed Shining Path militants, who, in turn, killed the police and the soldiers; and so were the children, forced into situations in which they killed and raped; and so were the torturers, poor young people who had to burn hundreds of cadavers and bury them behind the barracks so that no one would ever find them; and so were the Shining Path commands who—as punishment training, or a way to save bullets—stoned their enemies to death in the countryside and in neighborhoods, broken bone upon broken bone.

Where can enemies see their reflection? Is it in two parties' mutual understanding of their shared, wretched fate? Is it in the slightest recognition that the other has suffered, too? Is it in the absurdity of a world order that turns us into the murderous shadows of other bodies like ours? In 1918, shortly before he died, Wilfred Owen wrote this lucid, perhaps unfinished poem, in which he recognizes his enemy in a trench, which is hell:

Then, when much blood had clogged their chariot-wheels
I would go up and wash them from sweet wells,
Even with truths that lie too deep for taint.
I would have poured my spirit without stint
But not through wounds; not on the cess of war.
Foreheads of men have bled where no wounds were.

"I am the enemy you killed, my friend.
I knew you in the dark: for so you frowned
Yesterday through me as you jabbed and killed.
I parried; but my hands were loath and cold.
Let us sleep now. . . ."[4]
–

My enemy, submerged in me, commingled with me, sleeps, because in practice, that enemy is merely another form of my being.

63   I think about some of the people from MOVADEF who had to reinvent their lives after they got out of jail—not starting from zero, but rather facing the denial of their humanity. Their need for networks, support, and acceptance is like what any prisoner experiences at different times but is perhaps even more acute. In some cases, even their families have rejected them. Hope is dangerous, Tim Robbins told Morgan Free-

---

4. Owen, *Collected Poems*, 35–36.

man when he was thinking about escaping in the 1994 film *The Shawshank Redemption*. But so is hopelessness, realizing that there's no way anything will ever be different.

That's why different organizations of former Shining Path prisoners exist—not just MOVADEF, but several of them. Former prisoners need to have spaces where others won't accuse them. They need shelter where they can find relief from the silence of imprisonment. And they need simple things such as work, references, and a daily routine.

Not everyone chooses to join these groups, and not everyone uses them in the same way. For many, they serve as support networks. For others, perhaps a minority (I'm not sure), the networks help them deal with tougher issues: they provide spaces in which former prisoners can cling to those who give sense to their lives and meaning to their past sacrifices. Or did they live in vain? I'm not talking about groups of intellectual luminaries, like José María Arguedas, when he was questioned by learned men; instead, these are needy men and women questioning themselves and who are questioned by the present we inhabit.[5]

Who were the most hardened people in the prisons? Were they also the toughest on the outside? Some of these militaristic, disciplined individuals are the same people who, facing the "ultimate test," didn't pass it. They broke under torture. They talked and gave up their comrades. What were the consequences of "talking"? Torture and death followed by more torture and death—because they talked! Because of this, their self-loathing never abates. Their flaws caused some of them, as a reaction, to become the most immovable hard-liners in the prisons, toeing the party line. Once they were free, they felt compelled to keep playing that role.

They're paying a price. Can they escape their fate? Shouldn't a fate such as this move us to compassion?

---

5. This is a reference to the famous reply by José María Arguedas in the 1965 roundtable about his novel *Todas las sangres* at the Instituto de Estudios Peruanos, when he was vigorously questioned by young social scientists. He defended himself by stressing that his life and understanding of indigenous peasants had value unto itself, which intellectuals didn't know how to appreciate: "How could this not be a testimony, if I saw it, I lived it? If this is not a testimony, then I have not lived, or I have lived in vain." Rochabrún, *La mesa redonda*, 38.

64   Emmanuel Levinas wrote about forgiveness and surrender, perhaps out of desperation.[6] I agree with him that there is no other way to confront this challenge. Maybe my forgiveness isn't worth anything because I don't hold a position of power. I haven't been granted the ability to vindicate anyone. I am an extension of the guilty, of those who must keep silent out of respect or in order to survive.

To forgive is to surrender completely to others, to place oneself in their hands. It's not about expecting something in return or a political outcome. It means abandoning oneself and having the will to welcome, to console, to let ourselves be taken by others, or to die in them. It shouldn't be a prideful act or a gift. It's an act of humility.

65   That's why even though forgiveness is a gift, it shouldn't be. It's a gift in the sense that forgiveness brings prestige; it's a system based on balance and reciprocity. But when people spoil forgiveness by using it to secure impunity, it becomes ludicrous, a bad word.

More than a gift, perhaps forgiveness should be understood as a painful loss, a difficult letting go that at the same time means completing oneself in another. I can't, however, find the words to describe this.[7]

66   Jordi Ibáñez tells a story about a Francoist soldier who claims, "I am a surrendered man," even though he's won the battle.[8] This paradoxi-

---

6. Levinas, *De otro modo*.

7. Maybe it's something like what Paul Ricoeur said about "difficult forgiveness." Ricoeur said that to contemplate forgiveness is, at the same time, to ponder the unforgivable so as to avoid easy, evasive forgiveness, so as to avoid claiming that only the victim can forgive. Difficult and active forgiveness doesn't try to erase an offense, nor does it disappear facts that can't be eliminated from history. Rather, difficult forgiveness reconfigures the sense of the present and future of that debt: one party will always remain uncompensated, and the other will always remain a debtor unable to repay his or her debt. This pact based on failure, and at the same time on forgetting the consequences and sense of the offense, is the closest we can come to mutual forgiveness (Ricoeur, *Memory*, 457–459). I think this is still too much of a reciprocal pact. Perhaps a less pretentious approach might be to expect nothing in return, not even a failed pact. Like Borges's Judas, one has to subject oneself to disgrace and reprobation to not deserve anything.

8. Ibáñez, *Antígona y el duelo*, 153–165.

cal act, the soldier's will to share the fate of the conquered, has inspired my thinking, though I still stumble through my thoughts.

I belong to the amorphous community of the conquered. From where I stand, what might I have to surrender? Perhaps any and all possibilities of using my story to justify revenge—that would be something. But that's not the answer I'm seeking because I've never felt that way. If I were to answer my question in that way, it would simply be a rhetorical move.

Maybe my need to surrender myself, to give myself over to others, is a form of forgiveness. No one needs to ask for or desire my forgiveness, nor should I even want to grant it. When I play back my parents' final moments in my head, the last thing I want to do is forgive those who killed them so cruelly. When I remember the stories of so many victims I met while traveling around the country, I also feel no inclination to forgive. Quite the opposite: I'm moved by the same indignation so many activists and victims' organizations feel.

Forgiveness has meaning only because I don't want to forgive—because I shouldn't, because no one has asked me to, or because my gesture would be rejected . . . because I imagine, clumsily and naively, that it might help to achieve peace.[9]

I know—my forgiveness is worthless. It won't help to secure peace. Even a thousand acts of forgiveness won't keep peace from dissipating in the blood of the thousands of people who crack daily, as if their bodies can no longer contain them. There's no peace in forgiveness—only the prolonging of surrender and a faith in others that won't ever be fulfilled.

67 My brother is cleaning the room we lived in at Villa María. We were last there in 1998, fifteen years ago.

Sometimes, especially in difficult moments, I've disavowed that shady

---

9. This, despite Derrida's stern warning: "Every time pardon is at the service of a purpose, no matter how noble and spiritual (liberation or redemption, reconciliation, salvation), every time it reestablishes normalcy (social, national, political, psychological) through the work of mourning, through some type of therapy or ecology of memory, the 'pardon' is thus not pure, nor is its concept. Pardon is not and should not be normal, or normative, or normalizing. It should remain exceptional and extraordinary, put to the test of the impossible: as though you interrupted the ordinary course of historical temporality." Derrida, "Le siècle."

room, the only inheritance my parents left us. It's an abandoned place in a remote area that no one would ever want to buy. As an inheritance, it's useless because I'm never going to live there again anyway.

My parents were such capable people, so full of life. Yet even with all their ideas about justice, their urgent hunger for equality and solidarity, their charisma, and their unique, progressive qualities, they couldn't leave us anything more than this dump. Their idea of solidarity didn't help us, their children. But their vision of what a person might be willing to sacrifice did.

It's impossible not to think like this sometimes. It's impossible not to give in to the comfortable temptation to blame them for every misfortune or failure that life has thrown my way. Sometimes, especially on days like this, when I'm cleaning my room, it's tough to love them. It's like holding on to the living dead. I feel as if we've got to cure our bodies, delicately, in silence and with patience. We've got to forget—to forget a lot.

I'm not sure if I should call this tiny room a home because it was really a hideout, a safe place we'd go back to every time an emergency forced us to run. It all seems so naive now. But a couple of decades ago, hiding out there, in the shadow of the Atocongo Hills, gave us the feeling we were free of any danger, off the Lima grid, out of reach.

My parents set up this room when they were young, as if they were playing a game. They never had any intention of living here, nor do I now. Their home was in some future place, in a romantic utopia they knew they'd never live to see but that they hoped their children and grandchildren would see, along with everyone else's grandchildren.

I think my brother is going to take his time cleaning this room. Running toward the beach, as I do every summer, looking toward the sea, it has been a long time since I realized that the house my parents left me, this damned house, will never let me go . . .

. . . because the house lives in me.

A CONVERSATION WITH JOSÉ CARLOS AGÜERO

MICHAEL J. LAZZARA & CHARLES F. WALKER

How did your parents first get involved in Shining Path?

I always wanted an answer to that question. As a child, I often asked my mother about "the Party." She'd answer some of my questions, but to others she'd simply reply, "All in good time." She never told me in any detail about how she and my father got involved in Shining Path, but I can intuit certain things based on what I know.

My mother didn't start out in Shining Path; she started out in the Communist Party in the late 1960s. At the time, she worked as a secretary to the leadership, probably for Jorge del Prado, the historic leader of the Party, and some of the other old-timers. But after a while she resigned because she made friends who were part of the New Left. These friends constantly made fun of the Moscovite Communists and began to include my mother in their jokes. She later started exploring Trotskyism but ultimately found herself drawn to the MIR. In reality, everyone who was part of the Left, broadly speaking, knew everyone else. It was one big, lower-middle-class world that really felt small.

While my mother was a militant in the MIR, she started participating in educating the masses, particularly guilds and small unions; to do that work, she traveled frequently to the highlands. In Huancayo, she became so immersed in her daily routine that she eventually lost touch with the MIR, which was a precarious party anyway. Losing touch with the party base and with her broader networks plunged her suddenly into dire financial need. She thought she might die of hunger! Usually the party base supports its people; so, cut off from the base, my mother found herself without money even to buy bread.

In a moment of doubt about what she'd do next, Marco Antonio Briones, a physics professor, and Sybila Arredondo, the same woman who would later marry José María Arguedas and who eventually had links to Shining Path, took my mother in.[1] My mother befriended Sybila and her daughter. Meanwhile, my father had fallen on similar hard times: he, too, found himself abandoned by his party and wandering from place to place in need of help. Coincidentally, he showed up in Huancayo, and it was there that he met my mother. They fell in love and moved in together. That was how their romance began—and also my father's militancy in the MIR.

My parents stayed in Huancayo for a while, and eventually my father began to take on more active roles in the MIR and the Metalworkers' Union. He worked his way up the ladder to become national secretary of that union, which was one of the largest and most important in Peru. He remained part of organizations that played a key role in the strikes the workers organized in 1977 and 1978 against the military dictatorship of General Francisco Morales Bermúdez. He managed to gain some power in those roles; that's why many of his friends remember him as a fervent activist.

How did your parents move from the MIR into Shining Path?

I have no idea! I can make assumptions in my father's case, but I really have no idea about how my mother found her way to Shining Path. As I said, my father was already a leader who had proven his worth. He'd studied mechanical engineering and metallurgy at UNI. People respected him for the role he'd played in two major labor strikes, one that succeeded and another that failed. Still, he soon found himself out of a job because he had shared union information with Shining Path.

My father was a man of action, always ready to take on greater degrees of responsibility. I think that Shining Path offered him that chance. Had another leftist group crossed his path, he might have gone in another direction. But the timing and circumstances were just right for him to join Sendero.

Did your mother get involved in Shining Path because of your father?

I'm not really sure. It's hard to say. To be honest, this has never been something I've had a particular interest in discovering—perhaps because on some level I don't want to know. My paternal grandmother always accused my mother of having steered my father to Shining Path—but that's an accusation I simply have no way of substantiating.

What I can say is that my father was educated, an intelligent guy who'd made it to university, but at the end of the day he was from the provinces, from Tarma. He was much more staunchly Maoist than my mother. In fact, I don't think my mother was ever really a hardened Maoist at all. She may have been so on the surface and certainly learned to talk the talk, but I'm not sure she was ever totally convinced. Her path into Sendero wasn't clear-cut or even necessarily logical.

My father liked *huaynos*, traditional Andean songs; my mother preferred polkas, tangos, and waltzes. Her friends, too, were much more diverse than my father's. She probably chose the MIR at first because of its cultural bent. So, I'm not quite sure how she wound up in Shining Path. She might have been influenced by my father. She was certainly a woman of action—just like him—and was probably waiting for an opportunity to contribute something more to the revolutionary cause. Shining Path offered her (and him) that chance.

It seems as if your mother had a tense, very complex relationship with her militancy in Shining Path.

She wanted to give herself over to the Party wholeheartedly. As a child, I sensed she was constantly trying to convince herself that she was meant to do what she was doing. I got that impression from discussions I overheard and from meetings I witnessed in which long, drawn-out debates about basic leftist doctrine would strike her as tedious. Those discussions must have been sheer torture for her! I'm certain my mother was bored to tears by so much of the chatter that took place. She loved literature—not just books published by Editorial Progreso, a Soviet Union publisher that distributed widely in Spanish, but all sorts of literature. To sit there and listen to a bunch of young guys prattle on about the manuscripts they were reading by the Shining Path leader Abimael Guzmán must have been excruciating. I know it was for me!

What I can say for sure is that joining Shining Path ultimately changed my mother's life—and not for the better. Had she never gotten involved with the Party, she probably would have become a singer, a magnificent contralto. And I'm not just saying that because she was my mother. She had a truly wonderful voice!

What was your daily life like growing up as the son of two Shining Path militants? You visited them both in different prisons, which curiously were important organizational centers for Shining Path. Prisons obviously marked their lives and your relationship with them as well.

My parents went to prison in late 1983, and that was a turning point for me. My memories to that point are largely positive. Even though my parents were already active Shining Path militants, I generally felt safe. Our house in Lima's San Martín de Porres district was humble, for sure, but full of life. We were poor, but within poverty there are levels. Some of our neighbors were completely destitute, but my father, for example, had a motorcycle. My grandmother would cook big pots of food and share them with neighbors who didn't have enough to eat. Friends would come over all the time to ask advice, to borrow forks and knives, or to watch soccer matches because we had the only TV set in the neighborhood. At the time, my parents split their political involvement between Shining Path and union groups tied to the traditional Left. I remember times when our house would be full of people from the Metalworkers' Union or politicians who'd come over at night to brainstorm about how to recruit supporters. Militants would crash on our floor whenever they had nowhere else to go. I affectionately called them my tíos, my aunts and uncles. Years later, I'd see some of those same Shining Path militants again when I'd go to visit my father at El Frontón prison.

How did it affect your family when your father went to prison in 1983?

Things got tough for us economically. Our financial situation was already bleak in the months before my father was captured. His company had fired him for participating in a workers' strike. After that, his union networks helped him land a few subpar jobs, but none of them really kept us afloat. To make ends meet, he tried starting a few businesses on his own, such as one selling wooden toys out of an office he rented in downtown Lima, but he failed miserably at all of them. He was definitely no businessman! By that time, he had already become a Shining Path militant. He seemed torn between his business and waging the revolution. All of this, of course, caused lots of stress for my mother, who suddenly had to take financial responsibility for the family. To complicate matters further, my mother was also deepening her political involvements. In fact, I think the storefront where she worked selling beef imported from Chile may have doubled as a meeting point for Shining Path.

My father's imprisonment, though, had more than just a financial impact. As soon as he was arrested, we had to pack our bags and leave home. What's strange is that instead of going someplace where the police would never find us, we went to stay with my grandmother. Decisions like that, made on the fly, are difficult to justify or rationalize when I think back. But that's how things were.

In your book, you say that other people sometimes viewed you as an extension of your parents, as if you were "contaminated" by their political involvements. How did that make you feel?

To be fair, the situation wasn't always like that. Initially, I think people very much acted in solidarity with my parents and supported their beliefs. Many of our neighbors thought of my parents as courageous, leftist fighters. Hanging around my father and other militants gave me an early political education for which I'm very thankful. I'd listen intently to their conversations. I'd look at propaganda that my father would bring into the house. I'd ask him if his flyers were for the unions or for one of the left-wing political parties. Looking back, I'm grateful for the horizontal relationship I shared with my dad; he taught me to read even before I went to school.

After my father went to prison, however, things changed. I had to learn to tell lies, which went against the moral values my parents instilled in me. I hated lying, but I had no choice. I learned to make excuses whenever people asked me where my father was. "He went on a trip," I'd say. And I wasn't the only one who had to lie! My whole family had to do it. We learned to keep secrets—and to keep secrets is to acknowledge implicitly that something is wrong. The headmistress at school would look at me suspiciously and treat me unfairly simply because she knew my father was in prison. When my mother was taken to prison, too, just a few short months after my father, my feelings of being isolated and judged only grew stronger. Sometimes even extended family members would shun me. I had a cousin, for example, who was a classmate of mine and who'd go out of his way to let the teacher know that *he* wasn't part of a "terrorist" family. He was always trying to defend himself. Most of my extended family members who acted like this weren't doing it malevolently. They were simply trying to protect themselves.

The same sort of thing happened with my friends. I'd go to their houses to play, but they wouldn't let me in because their parents had forbidden it. My friends would feel bad turning me away. I'd usually let them off the hook gently by saying something like, "Don't worry. We'll do it another time."

Your father was taken first to the Lurigancho prison and later to El Frontón. Your mother was imprisoned in Chorrillos. What were your impressions of those places?

Peru's prisons were a major discovery for me! You had to get used to their protocols, their logic: you could visit women on Saturdays and men on Sundays. You could bring in only certain clothing or personal items as gifts for the prisoners. All of this, as a child, expands your world in a way that's jarring.

Lurigancho was a horrendous, abject place. Hellish, really! My father was held in the "industrial pavilion," where they kept Shining Path militants. But to get there, you first had to pass through the common prisoners' area, which smelled awful and looked completely dilapidated. It was unbearable! The guards, too, were brutal, always humiliating the prisoners.

When we'd go to visit my father, he'd usually be busy with tasks that Shining Path made him do. That's why he sometimes couldn't spend any time with us. Other prisoners, with Sendero's orders, would take responsibility for entertaining the families. Adult visitors might be bombarded with political lessons while kids watched some kind of play or ate lunch. None of it was pleasant.

Lurigancho was horrendous, but visiting my mother at Chorrillos was worse, maybe because I visited her more often. The prison itself was actually nicer: it had expansive common areas with trees and benches, and the women's cells were left open during visiting hours. The common prisoners loved my mother because she stood up for them. Shining Path women, by contrast, treated her coldly. That's why my mother saw to it that we spent the majority of our time with the common prisoners whenever we'd visit. Still, we couldn't avoid the Shining Path women. They'd act nasty toward my mother and mistreat us just to get back at her. I knew my father was in an awful place, but I honestly feared more for my mother, especially when she decided to help the common prisoners organize an uprising to defend their rights.

At first, my mother hoped to forge a united front between the political prisoners and the common ones. They all lived in squalor, and she believed that they all had a right to defend their basic needs. She wanted the prison guards to treat visitors better; she wanted them not to confiscate gifts that families brought for their loved ones. And she wanted every prisoner to have a decent bed, not just a mattress on the floor. The problem was that the Shining Path women didn't think it made sense to stage an uprising for the sole purpose of defending the prisoners' basic human rights. For Shining Path, any uprising had to have a loftier political purpose. Still, my mother stuck to her guns and went ahead with the plan anyway.

One day the common prisoners staged their mutiny. They barricaded their cells from the inside with beds and mattresses. They stuffed cushions in the windows. The Shining Path women begged my mother not to go through with it. They were scared! And, of course, the prison guards retaliated harshly. They set fire to the mattresses and cushions to force the women out of their cells. They mistreated many of the common prisoners but let them off the hook with comparatively light punishments. Because my mother was the leader, however, she paid a hefty price. They tortured her brutally in a remote area of the prison, and, to make an example out of her, they beat her senseless in front of the other women. My mother felt betrayed because she always had a good relationship with the prison warden, who was a woman. But in this case the warden turned a blind eye to the guards' punishments. After that, the common prisoners gave my mother the cold shoulder. They perhaps felt betrayed because they expected their demands would be met. The Shining Path women insisted that my mother had gotten the punishment she had coming.

I remember going to visit my mother after things took a turn for the worse. No one would speak to her. She appeared lonely, isolated, beaten down. I could sense that she knew exactly what she was putting us through, even if unintentionally. As a balm for our suffering, she bought us a few little cakes with a couple of coins she managed to get her hands on. I'm not sure where she got the money, but she spent them on a tiny gesture, a gift for her children. She must have convinced one of the guards to let her pass because we suddenly saw her come running toward us as we were leaving the prison. She practically forced the cakes into our hands and didn't say anything when she did.

I could understand how desperate she was, her desire that we not go home worried, her need to give us something—anything—as if to say, "I can't let you leave empty-handed or so concerned about me." It was shortly after that that they transferred her to the Callao prison as punishment for staging the uprising.

You mention in your book that you don't think it's fair for children to inherit their parents' guilt. But you also put some focus on your own small acts of complicity with your parents' militant actions: carrying documents, loading dynamite cartridges, and so forth. Do those little acts of complicity still bother you today, or do you think that you've come to terms with the role you played as a child?

Those things no longer cause me any moral angst because I've acknowledged that I did them. For me, acknowledging one's actions is a key step toward resolving any ethical matter. I know that what I did was wrong, even though I was also a victim. The fact that I was just a child when I did them, however, doesn't absolve me of responsibility for my actions.

These are tough issues! The fact is that I collaborated. I wasn't a naive kid. I was smart, cultured, and highly political. My house was a democratic place where information circulated freely. Certainly, I wasn't so acutely aware of what I was doing as to understand how my involvement in Shining Path's activities compared to other forms of leftist political activity.

Sure, it would be easy for me to use rhetoric to paint myself as a naive child who had no idea of what he was doing. But that would be a lie! It might be comfortable for me to say that, but I wouldn't be acknowledging honestly how things really were or what I understood or felt about them. So, yes, I believe I collaborated, with all my limitations. That collaboration was probably unwitting to some extent. But some of the things I did were definitely not child's play: they were part of chains of events that I'm sure caused much harm. I wasn't playing with dynamite cartridges thinking they were Play-Doh. I knew they were dynamite cartridges, and I knew that they would be used to blow up structures or kill people. Perhaps at the moment I was loading those cartridges it was hard for me to imagine what the scene would look like after they'd been detonated. I couldn't envision the mutilated bodies. But I did know that the explosives would be used for some purpose. Writing and speaking publicly about these issues is part of my process of resolving them.

Nevertheless, some issues are still difficult for me to resolve. I'll give you a good example. One night, a wounded man showed up at our house. He wasn't someone we knew well—only vaguely—and he was in bad shape. My mother was at home with a couple of her comrades, but the two comrades left the house quickly out of fear. My mother kept saying that someone was going to have to alert others about the potential danger; of course, she would never have expected me to do it. But I was the only one there. So, I volunteered to do what was needed and get the man out of our house, to protect both us and him. I was afraid he'd bleed out. I asked my mother for an address to which I could take the man for safety. I knew my neighborhood like the palm of my hand, so I was able to find the address she gave me.

I dragged the man out into the street at night and went in search of a potential safe haven. We hardly exchanged a word. He wasn't someone I'd seen more than twice in my life. He was scared, petrified. It's hard to say how old he was—maybe forty-five, perhaps younger because he was wounded and bleeding, patched up with a makeshift bandage. I must have been ten years old, almost eleven. At any rate, I got him to the house where I thought he'd be safe. The next day, however, I found out he was dead. The police had detained him and everybody else in the house. However, he was the only one they killed. The rest went to jail. The police later planted the man's body at a crime scene to make it look as if he had been killed in an armed confrontation.

What do you think would have happened to you had the police found you there in that moment?

Probably nothing.

You don't think they would have harmed you?

All of this happened in Lima. Had this scene played out in a rural community, the police likely would have killed everyone. But in Lima, they probably would have detained me, taken me to DINCOTE, and ultimately let me go—although they may have given me a good beating first.

The point is that ever since this happened, I've always felt as if I delivered that man to his death. Because it's true! Had the guy stayed the night at our house, or had he stayed until another adult showed up, or had we managed to find some other solution, he would never have wound up dead. I was the one who took him to that house where, unfortunately, the police staged a raid and killed him.

I don't remember the man's name, but his death still haunts me. I feel like—I'm not sure what I feel. I'm only sure that things shouldn't have turned out that way.

Is it difficult for you to accept what happened that night because you were ultimately trying to save the man?

What does it matter? In the end, they killed him.

Your book is not really about your parents primarily. It's dedicated to them, of course, but its main purpose isn't to recount their biographies or even discuss their militancy in depth. Really, the book is about you, about certain themes such as guilt, complicity, and victimhood that inspire your reflection. What role did you hope your parents would play as protagonists of your book? What is their place in your text?

They're a pretext—the pretext for a conversation. I know this is the case. And knowing that has emotional, moral, and ethical consequences for me. I know that I'm using them. And in every act of using someone there's always some degree of violence.

It's clear that your parents' militancy in Shining Path was very hard on you at times (and continues to be). Such an intense life—keeping secrets, always living on the edge, enduring extreme financial hardship and even prison—must have also taken a toll on them and their relationship.

After my mother staged the prison uprising, she got into a dispute with the "Party committee." Shining Path decided to sanction her. But because she was such a fighter, it wasn't something she was willing to take lying down. She got into a major conflict with the Party delegates;

I think the matter got discussed at some higher level of her committee. My mother never told me about any of this. I know it happened only because I've been able to reconstruct the episode partially from documents I've read and from a letter that my father sent to her.

My father wrote my mother a long letter that I read without her permission. In the letter, he expresses his concern for my mother but also speaks to her in a more formal tone on behalf of the Party. Seeing those two sides of him in one document made me uncomfortable. I would have expected him to have taken a different tone—a tone of solidarity, as if to say, "I'm with you to the death!" But that wasn't how he came across. Instead, my father said something like, "Think very hard about what you're doing. Be more careful. Don't be so combative. People are saying things about you behind your back." Bear in mind that my father was not a Shining Path leader, but he was part of the military cadre. That meant he had more rank and prestige than my mother within the Party structure. His letter was trying to convince her to stop her protests so that the Party would stop isolating her. In part, he was concerned about her; he feared that Shining Path would retaliate against her even harder. My mother told me much later that she had indeed received threats. At the time, she was dissatisfied with her relationship with the Party but also didn't like the pressure my father was putting on her. Their relationship was starting to break down.

Curiously, my parents were released from prison within a week of each other, in late 1984. Once we were all back at home together, living now in Villa María del Triunfo, my mother urged my father that they should quit the Party. By that time, they had both seen Shining Path's ugly side, so staying involved presented certain dangers. My mother had been branded a "bad militant"; she was angry at the Party for the extreme punishment it inflicted on her in prison. He accepted.

Yet as soon as we started to recover a little bit of normalcy the family was blindsided by a television report stating that my father had been detained again. He'd lied to my mother. He'd broken his promise and had gotten involved with Shining Path again—not in a tangential way but as an organizer. He was arrested while attempting to disarm a police officer. The operation resulted in a Hollywood–style chase around Lima that ended in the death of that police officer. They took my father to El Frontón prison, which just about destroyed my mother. She felt betrayed. It's hard to say why he got involved in the

Party again, why he broke his promise to my mother. It could have been his deep commitment to the Party, or maybe it was a function of his driven personality.

Your mother must have had a heavy burden to carry as head of the family and the spouse of a political prisoner.

On the one hand, she had to do whatever it took to make ends meet. In 1984 and 1985, for example, she made money taking people's blood pressure in the street in downtown Lima; I suspect that she did that not just to make money but also to recruit and build networks for Sendero. In moments when she was unemployed, the Party provided food and basic goods for our family. On the other hand, because she was the spouse of a political prisoner, Shining Path had certain expectations of her. As much as she may have wanted to steer clear of the Party, it obliged her to take on certain roles. For example, she participated in an organization of victims' families called Socorro Popular (Popular Aid) that later developed links to the most horrifying armed faction of Sendero. That association, I think, sealed her fate.

In an ideal world, my mother would have wholeheartedly supported the revolution. But in practical terms, I think that she regretted certain things she had to do as she got pulled deeper into Shining Path.

When I think about my parents, what I've realized over time is that they probably weren't exceptional. They were just average Peruvians, much like many other couples living at that time and in that context. They were both in Shining Path. They were married. But they were also very different from one another insofar as they exemplified two different kinds of militancy. As militants, they had different ways of relating to work, played different roles within the Party, and behaved differently in prison. My father assumed certain leadership roles within the Party, while my mother was more of a dissident. Both of them were people of action, but I imagine that my father was a little bit more so.

Like any normal couple, my parents had their problems. Around the time that my father deceived my mother about leaving the Party, she discovered that he was seeing another woman, a younger woman with two kids. My mother was, of course, furious but suggested that they move on as part of the new leaf they were turning over: they'd leave the Party and start to focus on their relationship and family. But my father didn't hold up his end of the bargain on either front. He kept seeing the other woman. And when my mother found out about it, she went ballistic. She called him a hypocrite, a dirty Maoist; she questioned whether he was a real revolutionary because he was clearly incapable of keeping his word. She threatened to leave him.

When that scene happened, I remember that my father and I were playing chess. As we sat in front of the chess board, I saw a tear roll down his cheek. My mother insisted it was a crocodile tear. As I look back, I think he probably loved that other woman, but my mother mattered to him, too. He certainly didn't hate my mother; in fact, I know he still loved her on some level. It was in that very moment that I realized how weak my father was. So, I moved my pawn. It was a terrible move—the worst move in the history of chess! But making it was like throwing him a lifeline. He knew exactly what I was doing and smiled at me thankfully. After that, he got up and headed toward the door. My brother and I ran after him, crying, begging him, "Don't go, Papá! Don't go!" That made my mother even more furious: "Look at what you're doing to these kids. You're making a bourgeois scene!" My father stopped cold in his tracks and decided to stay.

My father's relationship with that other woman was one of many cases in which imprisoned Shining Path men started relationships with women who were sent to visit them as part of Shining Path's prison support networks. Quite often those women would fall in love with the prisoners. They'd eventually join the support networks or the Party itself, become staunch supporters, and end up in jail. My father's mistress became deeply enmeshed in Shining Path because of her connection to my father. Eventually she got captured and spent more than ten years in the Canto Grande prison.

As things got progressively tougher on your mother and the family, did you try to convince her to abandon Shining Path?

Yes, absolutely! She tried to convince herself for a long time that Shining Path was the right choice for her—so much so that I think she wound up believing it. In a way, I don't think she could imagine any other options in life. At a certain point, she knew she was going to die. It was obvious to me that she sensed it. And she was very sad. We, of course, always knew her death was a real possibility. But she was certain of it—so certain, in fact, that she started talking to some of her comrades, asking them to help get her affairs in order in case the worst were to happen. I'm not saying that she had a death wish. I actually think she loved life. But at a certain point there was nothing more that could be done.

From 1985 until her death in 1992, my mother worked in a little kiosk at the University of San Marcos, which also served as a meeting point for radicalized students. My uncle owned the kiosk and gave my mother a job typing student papers. I would often go with her to work. The university was full of infiltrators just waiting to rat people out who had links to Shining Path. My mother died in 1992, but by 1991 the university had become solidly overrun by the military. One day, some soldiers entered the store where my mother was working. She knew immediately that she was screwed. They looked her over and snapped photographs; it was as if she were just waiting, waiting for the moment she'd be taken away.

My mother's death was one of a series of select, targeted killings of that took place between May and November 1992. There were roughly fourteen hundred murders of Shining Path militants during those months. By that time, most of the original members of Sendero were dead or captured. But a younger group of militants had formed in the meantime. Around 1991, the military started hunting down these younger militants while also going after the Party leadership. The military's witch hunt against Sendero was largely retaliatory: the army was furious with Sendero for having managed to keep the upper hand for so long. Shining Path would constantly mock the military and was much better organized and more disciplined than they were at El Frontón. The military felt humiliated, so it methodically exacted vengeance on Sendero during those months. There were thousands of detentions in those years, including a lot of innocent people.

Let's turn our attention to your book. How long did it take to write it?

It took at least ten years. At first, I had lots of fragments jotted down, lots of notes. A long time passed before I realized that it could all come together organically as a book.

When I finally decided to write the book, I knew only one thing for sure: I didn't want my biography to be the focal point. Instead, I hoped to talk about certain themes that I thought were important for understanding Peru's postconflict situation: shame, forgiveness, victimhood, guilt, stigma, and so on. To achieve this, I had to sort through many anecdotes, some of which I knew would work better than others to make the points I wanted to make. I also had to cut stories that people hadn't authorized me to share. My world is full of people from Shining Path and the MRTA who are constantly telling me about their experiences. I didn't feel I had a right to share their memories without permission, although in some cases I did ask them for permission.

When I recount their stories (or mine), I don't do it with a historian's attention to detail. Rather, my goal is to capture the deeper meaning behind encounters and episodes. When it came to certain personal stories, I simply chose to leave them out because I feared that telling them would be too hard on my family.

Public reactions to you have been somewhat mixed in Peru. The book has sold very well and sparked broad discussion. Yet some people label you a terrorist because of your association with your parents. Others have wanted to turn you into the spokesperson for all children of Senderistas. How do you respond to other children of Shining Path militants who want you to speak on their behalf?

The situation you're talking about is very real for me. It happens all the time. I've spoken to many other children of Shining Path militants who ask me to attend their meetings or to talk with them. They tell me they're happy that I'm giving them a voice. I usually reply, "I think it's great that you feel that way. Let's keep the conversation going. But I don't represent you." I don't put it so bluntly, of course, but I normally say something like, "We all have our own stories. Mine is unique, as I'm sure yours is. We're all different."

I'm not in favor of creating an organization of children of Senderistas. Although there are clear advantages to these kinds of organized groups—such as HIJOS in Argentina—such groups also limit our ability to think critically. On the one hand, they encourage an organized and very important societal defense of human rights, but on the other hand, they create circumscribed identities that can impede critical conversation. It's difficult to talk to people in groups such as HIJOS if you are not 100 percent in agreement with their political and ethical positions.

In Peru, the children of MRTA militants have been much more active than the children of Shining Path. They have their own HIJOS organization, which mirrors others that exist throughout Latin America. On several occasions, they've invited me to engage with them and have asked me to be their spokesperson. I can sense their pain and that they need support. I think that my book provides some of the support they're seeking because it dares to say things they'd like to say but that they've been reluctant to mention publicly. I'm always brutally honest with them. I tell them that while their experiences and mine share common elements, we also have important differences.

What impact has your book had on people in your immediate circle?

A particular case comes to mind. A mother who'd been in Shining Path and who was serving time in prison had a very strained relationship with her daughter. The daughter resented her mother for having abandoned her as a child to wage the revolution. At a certain point, the daughter stopped visiting her mother in prison and felt guilty because of it.

One day, the daughter asked to get together with me to chat. When we met, I gave her a copy of my book, which she later shared with her mother. Her mother read the book while still in prison, and it made her reflect deeply on her life. Soon thereafter things got much better between the mother and the daughter. The situation wasn't by any means perfect nor was it resolved forever, but the mother and daughter were minimally able to forgive one another.

Reading my book gave the mother an opportunity to tell her daughter that she understood the mistakes she'd made while in Sendero; likewise, the book opened a pathway for the daughter to work through the guilt, resentment, and rage she'd felt toward her mother for so many years. The daughter realized that she didn't have to forgive the state or its security forces for putting her mother in prison. She could still harbor resentment against the Peruvian state. The real perpetrator, for her, was her mother: it was her mother who had caused her harm and her mother whom she had to forgive. My book provided an opportunity for that process to take place.

Sometimes, too, situations arise that are difficult for me to handle. Once I was approached by a man whose father had been a Shining Path militant who'd killed a police officer in 1986. The man wanted to reach out to the children of his father's victim and asked me if I thought it would be a good idea to approach them. He had credible information that his dad had killed the officer in self-defense and wanted to ask their forgiveness.

To be honest, I'm not really sure what he should do. I know that for things to go well, the family would have to be willing to receive the man's reconciliatory gesture. To ask forgiveness of someone when that person isn't open to forgiving can be taken as an act of violence.

Your book gives the impression that armed struggle as a means to change society troubles you. Your parents belonged to a generation in Latin America in which many people turned to violence as a way to create radical systemic change, as a means to abate long-standing patterns of social, racial, ethnic, and economic discrimination and inequality. When you think about your parents and about the deep inequality that many Latin American societies still face today, how do you understand the idea of armed struggle?

Your question, of course, evokes an age-old discussion about the line between politics and violence. Personally, I reject the use of armed struggle as a way of dealing with societal problems. I'm certain I feel this way because I'm a child of postconflict—so my stance on this matter has to be contextualized with that in mind. I think that most people of my generation would have similar feelings on the matter. Perhaps that's logical.

What concerns me about the pacifist position, however, is that it can breed conservatism and impede movement toward social change. By rejecting armed struggle, one risks implicitly delegitimizing any form of radical protest. To reject armed struggle can therefore be discursively, politically, and ideologically disarming. If, as has happened in Peru, we manage to think about a very complex period of armed struggle as pure terrorism, we necessarily wind up thinking about every aspect of armed struggle as profoundly negative.

The contemporary global discourse on antiterrorism has left us orphaned. Antiterrorist paranoia has managed to disarticulate just about every expression of radical dissent by delegitimizing protest and reducing it to pure barbarism. In the end, I'm concerned that hard-line pacifism might result in the prolongation of many kinds of injustice.

Your book humanizes and demystifies many aspects of the Peruvian armed internal conflict. But even so, some silences and fictions probably remain. Are there zones of experience that are still difficult for Peru to address?

Peru needs proof! It needs evidence! As in other countries, we Peruvians live immersed in fictions. These fictions are not bold-faced lies but rather evasions. Fictions are strategies for evading hard truths. There are still people in Peru who walk around saying things like, "Get that terrorist out of here! Bring in the military, the heroes, to restore order!" And they can say these things because it hasn't yet become ingrained in people's hearts and minds that Peru's state security forces acted like cruel assassins. Sendero militants weren't the only ones!

Yet Sendero, too, acted with extreme cruelty. Former members of Shining Path, their families, and MOVADEF must also accept their share of responsibility. They have to help clarify the fate of those who disappeared at Shining Path's hands. They have to stop denying. Like the military, they have to help clarify details about armed actions, killings, and major massacres. This won't ever happen, however, unless people linked to Shining Path are given opportunities and safe spaces in which to speak.

If I were a government minister, I would work to create new laws that can help ease the return of former Shining Path members to functional roles in society. I can certainly understand why they have been shunned. But we're not talking about a few people. We're talking about lots of people! They all have lives, families, and personal agendas. They can't remain targets of resentment and scorn forever.

This country needs proof! It needs truth! It needs evidence of its cruelty! Peruvians can't simply pretend that they didn't act with extreme cruelty. The country has to prove to itself over and over again that it was terribly cruel. We can't just keep avoiding the blood staining our hands.

What's needed, then, to construct proof, to aid in Peru's process of self-reflection?

I think there are lots of ways to achieve it, but one important way is to share experiences. Sharing experiences doesn't mean making speeches or spinning tales. It means creating spaces in which meaningful and even difficult exchanges can happen peacefully and freely—without censorship and with openness to transformations of meaning in the process. That's what I hope to achieve with my work. If I were to articulate my own critical-cultural project, I'd say it's to facilitate the sharing and exchange of experiences.

Your comment leads to a tough question. Do you think it is the duty of children of Senderistas or of former Senderistas to investigate the details of their parents' deaths or of crimes their parents might have committed? Is it essential that we know who killed whom or who planted a bomb? This is an extremely delicate topic for those connected to Shining Path.

If we are going to pass strict moral judgments, in theory it is necessary to know details. It's one thing to have a general notion of evil and quite another to give that evil a name or a face. A child of someone who committed a crime could easily say, "I know that my father or mother did things, but he or she did them for good reasons." There's a danger in that. Thorough moral judgment requires facing up to reality.

We need more details, more family stories. The narratives that children of Senderistas tell depend to a great extent on the narratives they heard in their family circles. If they have always talked about their parents as heroes, they might not want to know the real truth. If we were to get one hundred children of Shining Path militants together, I would bet that half of them would tell romanticized, epic stories, whereas the other half might tell more ambiguous, reflective versions.

Ponciano del Pino talks about the "impurities of war." Reading your book and other histories of the Peruvian conflict gives the impression that despite Shining Path's absolutist politics and stories of heroes and villains, impurity dominated the conflict in just about every moment. But it's hard to admit impurities when it comes to the family or one's own autobiography. People tend to prefer versions that are more black and white.

It's fashionable to talk about "gray zones."[2] Researchers tend to read the Peruvian conflict's gray zones or impurities through a broad historical lens that contextualizes the conflict and its ambiguities. Although that approach is valid, I have a bit of a problem with it because I think it misses something important: that we also need to look carefully at the individualized, personal aspects of the conflict. Shining Path did not kill people indiscriminately. It killed people because of long-standing interpersonal conflicts rooted in particular locales.

We need to account for the localized nature of the violence—its day-to-day scenes—if we are ever to grasp the conflict's real dynamics. Sweeping metaphors such as *gray zones* and *impurities* block our perception of what motivated specific people in specific moments and contexts.

You have spoken out against "epic" narratives that create heroes, victims, martyrs, and villains. One of the great ironies, however, is that many people in Peru have wanted to label you a hero, a martyr, or a terrorist. How have you responded to this kind of labeling?

You always have to follow your conscience. People are constantly trying to label you so that they can control you. The fact that I won Peru's National Literary Prize for nonfiction in 2018 earned me the label of "noted writer." That's exactly the opposite of how I want to be seen. What have I really done as a writer? I've said some things that perhaps hadn't been said publicly, and I didn't sugarcoat my words. That's all. I also don't like when people label me—whether it be as a prize-winning writer, a terrorist, a hero, or a voice that speaks for all the children of Senderistas.

Epic narratives serve power—even when that power is weak. Epics construct fictions and myths of origin; they construct historical characters; they erect mausoleums. But who gets left out of those epics? We do. Epics make no room for critique and eclipse the lives of real people.

Do you consider your book an act of dissidence in the Peruvian context?

Absolutely! It's the act of dissidence that I can muster—heterogeneous, multiform, inorganic. I express experiences that can't be easily talked about in an orderly fashion—though maybe it isn't necessary to talk about everything in an orderly way.

Forgiveness is one of your book's major themes. The Peruvian situation, we know, is complex. The line between victims and perpetrators can be blurry. Sometimes it's unclear who should forgive whom—or for what. You spoke earlier of a dire need for proof in Peru. If, as you say, proof of the horror is still lacking in certain ways, even despite the monumental work that the TRC did, how can there be forgiveness without truth?

Forgiveness is imperfect. People are imperfect. The human subject can't produce anything, culturally speaking, that isn't imperfect—nothing that isn't on some level a failure, a step backward, a trace of doubt or uncertainty. Forgiveness is full of uncertainty—but that doesn't make it a mistake. That would be my practical answer to your question.

I'd like to think that I could forgive former president Alan García for ordering the prison massacre that resulted in my father's death. Forgiving him would no doubt have a series of positive effects on me. But would that act of forgiveness mean that I don't want justice served? No!

I'm not going to tie myself to any hard-and-fast rules. I don't seek revenge, nor do I want to look for my father's remains. I'm not interested in that. I know he's dead, and that's what I've always been taught. I'm simply not interested in that search. At least that's what I think today. Tomorrow my opinion might be different.

I know that others don't feel the same way. They need physical proof; they need to see their loved ones' remains. At times, I think that maybe I'm being self-centered when I say that I don't need the same things that others need. I know they killed my father—tortured him, dismembered him, that his body is . . . I don't need to know where he is because I know that he's dead. Not knowing causes me no anxiety. But I know it has caused anxiety for others: my aunt, my uncle, my grandmother. My grandmother died, and I suspect she went crazy thinking about this.

Reconciliation is another difficult concept. In postconflict societies, critics often ask if reconciliation is possible or should even be a goal, particularly when truth and justice are lacking. Some truth commissions around the world specifically choose not to include the idea of reconciliation in their mandates.

I think we have to be modest in our ambitions. We can ask people for only what they're able to give. We shouldn't ask our poor societies to create martyrs, heroes, or saints—only citizens, which in and of itself is already a lot to ask. We should expect our societies to educate citizens with an ability to think critically about the realities they're living. Citizens can participate in the political process. They can practice solidarity or demonstrate a concern for others. But they can't be expected to participate in reconciliatory processes unless societies equip them with the tools to do so. Reconciliation requires acceptance as its precondition. As a society, we have to ask ourselves what we are willing to accept as valid.

In the Peruvian case, there are still lots of lingering questions. Was torture valid? Was severe repression by the military a tolerable method for eliminating terrorism? It seems that in our country it was! People were willing to accept retaliation as a price to be paid for eliminating the terrorists.

As a society, are we willing to accept, too, that people have spent thirty years searching for the remains of their disappeared loved ones? Are we willing to accept that finding the disappeared is not yet public policy? In Peru, a commission was formed in 2016 to look for the disappeared.[3] Getting results will take years, and by that time many of those who are searching will have died. Maybe it will bring some peace to their children or grandchildren or serve as a lesson for future generations. But for the victims themselves, it won't do any good.

In the final assessment, I think we need to be much more reflective as a society. We all have to take charge of our baggage. But doing that is tough! To move forward, though, we have to accept the reality that we are living in a postconflict country: that there are crimes we still must acknowledge, that there are actions or omissions to which we still must admit, and that one of our first tasks as a society must be to create the institutional and societal conditions in which we can talk about difficult subjects without taboo. If we can't do that, reconciliation won't ever be viable. Yet it's still a worthwhile process that we need to set in motion if we ever hope to live just a little bit better.

Notes

1 Sybila Arredondo was married to the distinguished Peruvian writer and anthropologist José María Arguedas from 1967 until his suicide in 1969. In 1990 she was found guilty of being a member of Shining Path and spent twelve years in jail.

2 Here Agüero is referring to Primo Levi's concept that describes the horrifically complex ethical and political questions surrounding Jewish collaboration with the Nazis. Levi, *The Drowned*, 36–69.

3 Ley de Búsqueda de Personas Desaparecidas durante el Período de Violencia 1980–2000. Law #30470. June 21, 2016. Published in "Normas Legales," *El Peruano*, June 22, 2016.

BIBLIOGRAPHY

Agüero, José Carlos. *Cuentos heridos.* Illustrated by Andrea Lúrtura. Lima: Aguilar (Colección Lumen), 2017.
Agüero, José Carlos. *Enemigo.* Lima: Intermezzo Tropical, 2016.
Agüero, José Carlos. "La épica daña a toda sociedad democrática." Interview by Enrique Planas. *El Comercio* (Lima), December 18, 2017.
Agüero, José Carlos. *Persona.* Lima: Fondo de Cultura Económica, 2017.
Agüero, José Carlos. *Los rendidos: Sobre el don de perdonar.* Lima: Instituto de Estudios Peruanos, 2015.
Agüero, José Carlos, and Pablo Sandoval. *Aprendiendo a vivir se va la vida: Conversaciones con Carlos Iván Degregori.* Lima: Instituto de Estudios Peruanos, 2015.
Aguirre, Carlos. "Punishment and Extermination: The Massacre of Political Prisoners in Lima, Peru, June 1986." In *Murder and Violence in Modern Latin America,* edited by Eric A. Johnson, Ricardo Salvatore, and Pieter Spierenburg, 193–216. London: Wiley-Blackwell, 2013.
Aguirre, Carlos. "Terruco de m . . . : Insulto y estigma en la guerra sucia peruana." *Histórica* (Lima) 35, no. 1 (2011): 103–139.
Álvarez Rodrich, Augusto "Apología de la imbecilidad." *La República* (Lima), May 19, 2018. https://larepublica.pe/politica/1245580-apologia-imbecilidad.
Ames, Rolando, et al. *Informe al Congreso sobre los sucesos de los penales.* Lima: OCISA, 1988.
Aronés, Mariano. "'Si no matas, te matan': Memoria y drama del servicio militar en el contexto de la guerra interna en el Perú." Paper presented to the Grupo Memoria, Lima, 2012.
Asencios, Dynnik. *La ciudad acorralada: Jóvenes y Sendero Luminoso en Lima de los años 80 y 90.* Lima: Instituto de Estudios Peruanos, 2017.
Asimov, Isaac. "The Gentle Vultures." In *Nine Futures: Tales of the Near Future,* 120–136. New York: Doubleday, 1959.
Boesten, Jelke. *Sexual Violence during War and Peace: Gender, Power, and Post-Conflict Justice in Peru.* London: Palgrave Macmillan, 2014.
Burt, Jo-Marie. "Guilty as Charged: The Trial of Former Peruvian President Alberto Fujimori." *International Journal of Transitional Justice* 3 (2009): 384–405.

Burt, Jo-Marie. *Political Violence and the Authoritarian State in Peru: Silencing Civil Society*. New York: Palgrave Macmillan, 2008.
Cabrera, Teresa. *Sueño de pez o neblina*. Lima: Álbum del Universo Bakterial, 2010.
Comisión de la Verdad y Reconcilatión. *Informe final* August 28, 2003. https://www.usip.org/publications/2001/07/truth-commission-peru-01.
Comisión Investigadora de los Sucesos de Uchuraccay. *Informe de la Comisión Investigadora de los sucesos de Uchuraccay*. Lima: Comisión Investigadora, 1983.
Conaghan, Catherine. *Fujimori's Peru: Deception in the Public Sphere*. Pittsburgh, PA: University of Pittsburgh Press, 2005.
Congreso de la República del Perú. *La barbarie no se combate con la barbarie*. Lima: Congreso de la República del Perú, 1988.
Dagerman, Stig. *Nuestra necesidad de consuelo es insaciable*. Logroño: Pepitas de Calabaza, 2007.
Degregori, Carlos Iván. *How Difficult It Is to Be God: Shining Path's Politics of War in Peru, 1980–1999*. Madison: University of Wisconsin Press, 2012.
Degregori, Carlos Iván. *Obras escogidas de Carlos Iván Degregori*. 14 vols. Lima: Instituto de Estudios Peruanos, 2011–2016.
Degregori, Carlos Iván. *Qué difícil es ser Dios: El Partido Comunista del Perú-Sendero Luminoso y el conflicto armado interno en el Perú, 1980–1999*. Lima: Instituto de Estudios Peruanos, 2010.
Degregori, Carlos Iván. "Sobre la Comisión de la Verdad y Reconciliación en el Perú." In *No hay mañana sin ayer: Batallas por la memoria y consolidación democrática en Perú*, by Carlos Iván Degregori, Tamia Portugal Teillier, Gabriel Salazar Borja, and Renzo Aroni Sulca, 27–68. Lima: Instituto de Estudios Peruanos, 2015.
del Pino, Ponciano. *En nombre del gobierno: El Perú y Uchuraccay: Un siglo de política campesina*. Lima: La Siniestra Ensayos/Universidad Nacional de Juliaca, 2017.
del Pino, Ponciano, and José Carlos Agüero. *Cada uno un lugar de memoria: Fundamentos conceptuales del Lugar de Memoria, la tolerancia y la inclusión social*. Lima: LUM, 2014.
del Pino, Ponciano, and Caroline Yezer, eds. *Las formas del recuerdo: Etnografías de la violencia política en el Perú*. Lima: Instituto de Estudios Peruanos/Instituto Francés de Estudios Andinos, 2013.
Derrida, Jacques. "Le siècle et le pardon." Interview by Michel Wieviorka. *Le monde des débats* 9 (December 1999).
Feinstein, Tamara. "Competing Visions of the 1986 Lima Prison Massacres: Memory and the Politics of War in Peru." *A contracorriente: Una revista de estudios latinoamericanos* 11 (2014): 1–40.
Gálvez Olaechea, Antonio. *Desde el país de las sombras*. Lima: SUR, 2009.

Gavilán Sánchez, Lurgio. *Memorias de un soldado desconocido: Autobiografía y antropología de la violencia*. Lima: Instituto de Estudios Peruanos, 2012.

Gavilán Sánchez, Lurgio. *When Rains Became Floods: A Child Soldier's Story*. Durham, NC: Duke University Press, 2015.

Gelman, Juan. "Hay que moverse del lugar de la víctima." Interview by Patricia Garma. *Tico Visión: La Tribuna para el Libre Pensamiento*, February 7, 2013. www.ticovision.com/cgi-bin/index.cgi?action=viewnews&ia=12207.

Goffman, Erving. *Stigma: Notes on the Management of Spoiled Identity*. New York: Touchstone, 1986.

Gonzáles, Eduardo. "Nuevas fronteras para el ejercicio de la memoria en el mundo y en el Perú." Paper presented at El Seminario Internacional Políticas en Justicia Transicional, Lima, August 22, 2013.

González, Olga. *Unveiling Secrets of War in the Peruvian Andes*. Chicago: University of Chicago Press, 2011.

Gorriti, Gustavo. *The Shining Path: A History of the Millenarian War*. Chapel Hill: University of North Carolina Press, 1999.

Grass, Günter. *Selected Poems*. Translated by Michael Hamburger and Christopher Middleton. New York: Harcourt, Brace and World, 1966.

Ibáñez, Jordi. *Antígona y el duelo*. Barcelona: Tusquets, 2009.

Jebeleanu, Eugen. "Canto a los muertos desconocidos de Hiroshima." In *Breve antología de las poesía rumana*, 24. Lima: Humboldt, n.d.

Jelin, Elizabeth. *Los trabajos de la memoria*. Buenos Aires: Siglo Veintiuno de Argentina Editores/Social Science Research Council, 2002.

Juarroz, Roberto. "El silencio que queda entre dos palabras . . ." In *Poesía vertical: Antología esencial*, 269–270. Buenos Aires: EMECÉ, 2005.

Kundera, Milan. *The Unbearable Lightness of Being: A Novel*. New York: Harper Classics, 2009.

Levi, Primo. *The Drowned and the Saved*. New York: Simon and Schuster, 2017.

Levi, Primo. *La trilogía de Auschwitz*. Translated by Pilar Gómez Bedate. Barcelona: El Aleph, 2005.

Levinas, Emmanuel. *De otro modo que ser o más allá de la esencia*. Salamanca: Sígueme, 2011.

Llamojha Mitma, Manuel, and Jaymie Patricia Heilman. *Now Peru Is Mine: The Life and Times of a Campesino Activist*. Durham, NC: Duke University Press, 2016.

Manrique, Marie. "Generando la inocencia: Creación, uso e implicaciones de la identidad de 'inocente' en los períodos de conflicto y posconflicto en el Perú." *Boletín del Instituto Francés de Estudios Andinos* 43 (2014): 53–73.

Méndez, Juan. "Significance of the Fujimori Trial." *American University International Law Review* 25, no. 4 (2010): 649–656.

Milton, Cynthia, ed. *Art from a Fractured Past: Memory and Truth-Telling in Post-Shining Peru*. Durham, NC: Duke University Press, 2014.

Milton, Cynthia. *Conflicted Memory: Military Cultural Interventions and the Human Rights Era in Peru*. Madison: University of Wisconsin Press, 2018.

Oglesby, Elízabeth. "Educating Citizens in Postwar Guatemala: Historical Memory, Genocide, and the Culture of Peace." *Radical History Review* 97 (1997): 77–98.

Owen, Wilfred. *The Collected Poems of Wilfred Owen*. New York: New Directions, 1965.

Paz, Octavio, and Eliot Weinberger. "Interrupted Elegy." *Conjunctions* 57 (2011): 116–118.

PCP–Sendero Luminoso. "Sobre las dos colinas (Documento de estudio para el balance de la III Campaña)." 1991. http://library.redspark.nu/1991_-_Sobre_las_dos_colinas_(Documento_de_estudio_para_el_balance_de_la_III_Campa%C3%B1a).

Portugal Teillier, Tamia. "Batallas por el reconocimiento: Lugares de memoria en el Perú." In *No hay mañana sin ayer: Batallas por la memoria y consolidación democrática en Perú*, by Carlos Iván Degregori, Tamia Portugal Teillier, Gabriel Salazar Borja, and Renzo Aroni Sulca, 69–236. Lima: Instituto de Estudios Peruanos, 2015.

Qorawa, Miguel. "Prólogo." In *Memorial de trincheras I: Testimonios de prisiones*, 9–16. Lima: n.p., 2015.

Reátegui, Félix, ed. *Criterios básicos para un espacio de conmemoración de la violencia en el Perú: La centralidad de los derechos de las víctimas*. Lima: IDEHPUCP-Misereor, 2012.

Remarque, Erich Maria. *All Quiet on the Western Front*. New York: Ballantine, 1987.

Rénique, José Luis. *La voluntad encarcelada: Las "luminosas trincheras de combate" de Sendero Luminoso del Perú*. Lima: Instituto de Estudios Peruanos, 2002.

Ricoeur, Paul. *Memory, History, Forgetting*. Translated by Kathleen Blamey and David Pellaur. Chicago: University of Chicago Press, 2006.

Rochabrún, Guillermo, ed. *La mesa redonda sobre "Todas las sangres": 23 de junio de 1965*. 2nd ed. Lima: Instituto de Estudios Peruanos/Fondo Editorial de la Pontificia Universidad Católica del Perú, 2000.

Scorza, Manuel. *Redoble por Rancas*. Barcelona: Plaza y Janés, 1970.

Sikkink, Kathryn. *The Justice Cascade: How Human Rights Prosecutions Are Changing World Politics*. New York: Norton, 2011.

Soifer, Hillel David, and Alberto Vergara. *Politics after Violence: Legacies of the Shining Path Conflict in Peru*. Austin: University of Texas Press, 2018.

Starn, Orin, and Miguel La Serna. *The Shining Path: Love, Madness, and Revolution in the Andes*. New York: Norton, 2019.

Stern, Steve J., ed. *Shining and Other Paths: War and Society in Peru, 1980–1995.* Durham, NC: Duke University Press, 2002.

Stern, Steve J., and Peter Winn. "El tortuoso camino chileno a la memorialización (1990–2011)." In *No hay mañana sin ayer: Batallas por la memoria histórica en el cono sur,* edited by Steve Stern, Peter Winn, Federico Lorenz, and Aldo Marchesi, 261–410. Lima: Instituto de Estudios Peruanos, 2013.

Theidon, Kimberly. *Intimate Enemies: Violence and Reconciliation in Peru.* Philadelphia: University of Pennsylvania Press, 2013.

Todorov, Tzvetan. *Hope and Memory: Lessons from the Twentieth Century.* Princeton, NJ: Princeton University Press, 2003.

Torres, Javier. Interview by Elizabeth Jelin. *La Mula,* September 1, 2014. https://elarriero.lamula.pe/2014/09/01/con-la-nocion-de-victima-se-pierde-la-nocion-de-actor/javierto/.

Uccelli, Francesca, José Carlos Agüero, María Angélica Pease, and Tamia Portugal. *Atravesar el silencio: Memorias sobre el conflicto armado interno y su tratamiento en la escuela.* Lima: Instituto de Estudios Peruanos, 2017.

Uccelli, Francesca, José Carlos Agüero, Ponciano del Pino, María Angélica Pease, and Tamia Portugal. *Secretos a voces: Memoria y educación en colegios públicos de Lima y Ayacucho.* Lima: Instituto de Estudios Peruanos, 2013.

Uceda, Ricardo. *Muerte en el pentagonito: Los cementerios secretos del Ejército Peruano.* Bogotá: Planeta, 2004.

Ulfe, María Eugenia, and Carmen Ilizarbe. "El indulto como acontecimiento y el asalto al lenguaje de la memoria en Peru." *Revista Colombia Internacional* 97 (2019): 117–143.

Ulfe, María Eugenia, and Carmen Ilizarbe. "Paloma y acero: *Sibila.*" *Noticias* SER, October 11, 2013.

University of California, Davis, Hemispheric Institute on the Americas. "Shining Path 2016 HIA Agüero Gavilán." Conference discussion at Aftermath of the Shining Path: Memory, Violence, and Politics in Peru, February 11, 2016. Video, 1:06. Posted March 4, 2016. https://www.youtube.com/watch?v=k4NZyHWlIow.

Varela, Blanca. "Casa de cuervos." *Hueso Húmero* 4 (1980): 8–10.

Vich, Víctor. *Poéticas del duelo: Ensayos sobre arte, memoria y violencia política en el Perú.* Lima: Instituto de Estudios Peruanos, 2015.

Wiesel, Elie. *The Night Trilogy.* New York: Hill and Wang, 2008.

Youngers, Coletta. *Peru's Coordinadora Nacional de Derechos Humanos: A Case Study of Coalition Building.* Washington, DC: WOLA, 2002.

INDEX

Page numbers in italics refer to figures.

accomplices, 27, 67–71, 74, 115
Agüero, José Carlos: on armed struggle, 124; brother of, 8, 32n10, 33, 85n8, 105–7, 120; career of, 14–15; childhood, 1, 111–12, 113–15; on complicity and guilt, 115–17; on cruelty and proof, 125–26; on forgiveness, 128; grandmother of, 61–64, 102, 109, 112, 128; on "gray zones," 126–27; on judgments of others, 112–13; on parents, 108–10, 117–21; published works, 14–15; on reconciliation, 128–29; on *Los rendidos*, 122–24; on writing, 121–22, 127
Agüero Aguirre, José Manuel (José Carlos Agüero's father), 7–13; death, 12, 18n16, 93–94, 128; and MIR, 109; mistress of, 13, 56, 120; photograph, 8, 9; and police station attack, 10, 12, 58, 58n1, 60n2, 61, 93, 113, 118; and Shining Path, 10, 12, 108–13, 117–21; strike involvement, 10, *11*
All Quiet on the Western Front (Remarque), 35, 96
Amadeus (film), 65, 65n1
ancestors, 59–64
ANFASEP (Asociación Nacional de Familiares de Secuestrados, Detenidos y Desaparecidos del Perú), 70
"apologies for terrorism" laws, 2, 17n3
Aprendiendo a vivir se va la vida (Agüero and Sandoval), 14
Argentina, 43, 122
Arguedas, José María, 104, 104n5, 108, 130n1
Arredondo, Sybila, 108, 130n1
Arredondo, Teresa, 25n1, 36n18
Asimov, Isaac, 90
Asociación Nacional de Familiares de Secuestrados, Detenidos y Desaparecidos del Perú (ANFASEP), 70
Asociación pro Derechos Humanos, 7

Balbuena, Patricia, 2
Belaúnde, Fernando, 3
Benito (Agüero's childhood friend), 31, 31n8
Briones, Marco Antonio, 108

Cabrera, Teresa, 30
Cada uno un lugar de memoria (del Pino and Agüero), 15
Chamberlain, Neville, 90
Chorrillos prison, 8, 42, 113. *See also* prisons
civil war (term), 5
Comisión de la Verdad y Reconciliación. *See* TRC (Truth and Reconciliation Commission)
"Como cualquier peruanito" (Cabrera), 30, 30n6
compassion, 38, 38n20, 97, 101, 104
complexity: of guilt, 21, 52–53; of political life, 86; of violence, 92
complicity, 27, 67–71, 74, 115. *See also* guilt
Coordinadora Nacional de Derechos Humanos, 7, 69
Cuentos heridos (Agüero), 15
Cultural Revolution (China), 3, 75. *See also* Maoist movement

Dagerman, Stig, 97
Degregori, Carlos Iván, 14–15, 22n1, 53, 65
dehumanization, 99
del Pino, Ponciano, 15, 21–22, 84, 84n7, 126

Derrida, Jacques, 106n9
Dietrich, Martha, 97
DIRCOTE/DINCOTE (Dirección Nacional contra el Terrorismo), 43, 85, 116–17
Donayre, Edwin, 2

empathy, 14, 36–37, 36n18, 94
Enemigo (Agüero), 14
epic narratives, 7, 126, 127

fear, 51–52, 55, 56, 74, 83–84, 85n8, 99, 102
films: *Amadeus*, 65, 65n1; about prisons, 35–36, 103–4; *Shawshank Redemption*, 103–4; about Shining Path, 25–27, 25n1; *Sybila*, 36n18
forgiveness, 49, 54–55, 96, 98, 105–6, 105n7, 124, 128
El Frontón prison island, 13, 62, 63, 121; Agüero's father at, 10, 12, 58, 58n1, 60n2, 61, 93, 111, 113, 118; violence at, 12, 58n1, 60n2, 64, 102, 128. *See also* prisons
Fujimori, Alberto, 2, 4, 26n2, 98, 100–101
Fujimori, Keiko, 2, 4–5
Fujimori, Kenji, 4
Fujimoristas, 4–5, 99, 100

Gálvez Olaechea, Alberto, 48–49n6
García, Alan, 12, 18n16, 58n1, 64, 102, 128
Gavilán Sánchez, Lurgio, 1, 65–67, 69–70
Geneva Convention, 3
Goffman, Erving, 24
Gonzáles, Juan Carlos, 2
Gonzalo (Comrade/Presidente Gonzalo; Abimael Guzmán Reynoso), 4, 9–10, 33, 78, 110
Grass, Günter, 65
"gray zones," 84n7, 126–27
grief, 48, 101–2
guilt: inheriting, 50–51, 54, 55–56; relief and, 41–44; survivor, 44n3
Guzmán Reynoso, Abimael (Comrade/Presidente Gonzalo), 4, 9–10, 33, 78, 110

HIJOS (Hijas e Hijos por la Identidad y la Justicia contra el Olvido y el Silencio, Argentina), 122–23

Hodgson, William, 83
human rights, 5–7; Geneva Convention, 3; as nonnegotiable, 68, 91; organizations and activists, 6, 7, 14, 15, 34n14, 37, 70, 73, 98, 101, 122; paradigm, 80, 82; victims and, 80, 82, 89, 91, 92, 94. *See also specific organizations*
humiliation, 25, 55, 98, 100, 113, 121

Ibáñez, Jordi, 105–6
indigenous people, 4, 47, 66, 70, 104n5
innocent victims. *See* victims
Inter-American Court of Human Rights, 98
internal armed conflict (term), 5

Jebeleanu, Eugen, 88–89
Jelin, Elizabeth, 82

Kuczynski, Pedro Pablo, 4
Kundera, Milan, 38, 38n20

Levi, Primo, 44n3, 84n7, 98, 130n2
Levinas, Emmanuel, 105
Lima, Peru, 25–26, 27, 43, 63, 92; Agüero's family in, 9–10, 111, 119; El Agustino district, 31; *chicha* cultural melting pot, 37; *conos*, 34, 34n12; Moyano assassination, 47, 47n5; police in, 116–17, 118; prison riots in, 12; San Martín de Porres district, 111; violence in, 4, 6, 16, 33n11, 47–48, 85, 96, 100, 101, 107
LUM (Lugar de la Memoria, la Tolerancia y la Inclusion Social), 2, 5, 15, 84, 92
Lurigancho prison, 12, 71, 72, 102, 113. *See also* prisons

Mamá Angélica (Angélica Mendoza de Escarza), 37
Manrique, Marie, 68, 87n9
Maoist movement, 1, 3, 4, 6, 10, 110, 120
Memorias de un soldado desconocido (Gavilán Sánchez), 1, 65–67, 69–70
Memory Museum (LUM), 2, 5, 15, 84, 92
memory studies, 5, 15, 22n1
Memory Studies Workshop, 22, 22n2, 27n4

Mendoza de Escarza, Angélica (Mamá Angélica), 37
MIR (Movimiento de Izquierda Revolucionaria), 7–8, 108, 109, 110
Montesinos, Vladimiro, 4
Morales Bermúdez, Francisco, 3, 10, 109
moral superiority, 27, 59, 101
MOVADEF (Movimiento por Amnistía y Derechos Fundamentales), 2, 27, 27n3, 47, 99, 103–4, 125
Movement for Amnesty and Fundamental Rights (MOVADEF), 2, 27, 27n3, 47, 99, 103–4, 125
Movimiento Revolucionario Túpac Amaru (MRTA), 38, 48–49n6, 71, 97, 122–23
Moyano, María Elena, 47, 47n5
MRTA (Movimiento Revolucionario Túpac Amaru), 38, 48–49n6, 71, 97, 122–23
Mujica, José, 61
myth and mythologizing, 4, 26, 28, 36n18, 66, 97, 127

National Association of Relatives of the Kidnapped, Detained, and Disappeared in Peru (ANFASEP), 70
National Coordinator of Human Rights, 7, 69
National Directorate against Terrorism (DIRCOTE/DINCOTE), 43, 85, 116–17
National Engineering University (UNI), 10, 109
National Literary Prize, 7, 127
Nazism, 59, 90, 130n2
NGOs (nongovernmental organizations), 25–27, 47, 48, 67–70, 80n1, 81, 98

Obras escogidas de Carlos Iván Degregori (Agüero, ed.), 14–15
Owen, Wilfred, 103

Pardons Commission, 98
Paz, Octavio, 58
Persona (Agüero), 7, 14
Peruvian Communist Party. *See* Shining Path (Sendero Luminoso)

police, 50; Agüero parents and, 10, 30–33, 42, 49, 118; dehumanization of, 99; hiding from, 112; secret, 43, 43n1; torture by, 72; violence against, 10, 49, 118, 123; wounded man killed by, 116–17; youth of, 34
political prisoners, 27–28n4, 119
Premio Nacional de Literatura, 7, 127
prisons: Agüero parents in, 10, 12, 58, 58n1, 60n2, 61, 93, 111–15, 117–20; Chorrillos, 8, 42, 113; family members in, 42, 43, 103–4, 111, 123–24; films about, 35–36, 103–4; former prisoners, 103–4, 118; Lurigancho, 12, 71, 72, 102, 113; political prisoners, 27–28n4, 119; Santa Bárbara, 12, 102; Shining Path militants in, 27–28n4, 35, 47, 51, 56, 68; spouses of prisoners, 119–20; violence in, 12, 58n1, 60n2, 64, 68, 72, 102, 128; women prisoners, 36, 85, 85n8, 97. *See also* El Frontón prison island
public secrets, 30–31, 33

Qorawa, Miguel, 3

racism, 4, 28, 92
rage, 39, 56, 61, 123
Reátegui, Félix, 81n3
Los rendidos: Sobre el don de perdonar (Agüero), 1, 3, 5, 14–15
reparations, 37, 46, 53, 61, 81, 89, 90n12, 91, 91n13, 96, 97
revenge, 6, 10, 39, 40, 84, 93, 102, 106, 128
Revolutionary Left Movement (MIR), 7–8, 108, 109, 110
Ricoeur, Paul, 105n7

Sandoval, Pablo, 14
Santa Bárbara prison, 12, 102. *See also* prisons
Scorza, Manuel, 67
Sendero Luminoso. *See* Shining Path (Sendero Luminoso)
shame, 15, 24–25, 28–29, 44n3, 47, 55, 96, 121
Shawshank Redemption (film), 103–4
Shining Path (Sendero Luminoso), 25–27; Agüero's father and, 10, 12, 108–13, 117–21;

Shining Path (*continued*)
Agüero's mother and, 7–9, 108–10, 117–21; children and, 5, 29–30; Guzmán Reynoso and, 4, 9–10, 29–30, 33, 78, 110; imprisoned militants, 27–28n4, 35, 47, 51, 56, 68; indigenous people and, 4, 47, 66, 70, 104n5; "people's war" and, 3; terrorists and, 1, 46, 47, 47n5, 59, 125; violence in Lima, 4, 6, 16, 33n11, 47–48, 85, 96, 100, 101, 107

sin, 59. *See also* guilt

Solórzano Mendívil, Silvia (José Carlos Agüero's mother), 7–13; death, 9–10, 33, 33n11, 42, 44–45, 60, 78–79, 101–2; and MIR, 7–8, 108, 110; photograph, 8; and Shining Path, 7–9, 108–10, 117–21

Sons and Daughters for Identity and Justice against Oblivion and Silence (HIJOS, Argentina), 122–23

Space for Memory, Tolerance, and Social Inclusion (LUM), 2, 5, 15, 84, 92

stereotypes, 53, 84

stigma, 13, 24, 65, 98, 102, 121

Sybila (documentary), 36n18

Tapia, Segundo, 2

Tarata Street car bombing, 47, 47n5

terrorists and terrorism, 5; Agüero as, 14; Agüero's mother as, 8, 31, 33; antiterrorism, 124; "apologies for terrorism" laws, 2, 17n3; children of, 2, 8, 13, 15, 60, 64, 94, 97, 112–13; dignity and, 59; label, 2, 122, 127; military repression and, 129; oversimplification and, 6; Shining Path and, 1, 46, 47, 47n5, 59, 125; *terruca/terruco*, 32, 32n9, 46, 71, 86; victims and, 86, 91

testimony, 14, 45, 46, 62, 69, 92–93

Todas las sangres (Arguedas), 104n5

Todorov, Tzvetan, 37, 37n19

transitional justice, 59, 80n1, 81n3, 90

TRC (Truth and Reconciliation Commission), 45–48; Agüero and, 15; critics of, 5, 47–48, 89, 92; forgiveness and, 128; *Informe final*, 1, 16n1, 47n4, 81n3; on killing of journalists, 66n2; Reparations Council, 90–91; on sexual violence, 85n8

Trotskyism, 7–8, 108

truth: certainty of, 70; defining and valuing, 70; easy, 59; evading, 125; forgiveness and, 128; inability to tell, 24–25; need for, 125; of parents, 126; of the past, 39–40; responsibility and, 102; stories and, 25, 102; victims and, 92

truth commissions, 80n1, 128. *See also* TRC (Truth and Reconciliation Commission)

Tupac Amaru Revolutionary Movement (MRTA), 38, 48–49n6, 71, 97, 122–23

Tupamaros (Uruguay), 61

Uchuraccay massacre, 66, 66n2, 92

UNI (Universidad Nacional de Ingeniería), 10, 109

United Left, 57, 67

Universidad Nacional de Ingeniería (UNI), 10, 109

University of Ayacucho, 4

University of San Marcos, 9–10, 41–42, 49, 64, 121

Uruguay, 61

Varela, Blanca, 41

Vargas Llosa, Mario, 66, 66n2

Velasco Alvarado, Juan, 3

victim-centered approach, 80–82, 91–92, 97

victimization, 94

victims and victimhood, 60–61; artists and, 37; children as, 115; complicity and, 115; deconstructing, 92; families of, 37, 115, 119, 123–24; guilt and, 88; harm and, 89; heroes and, 59; humanization of, 6; of human rights violations, 53; innocent, 37, 80–81, 84n7, 92; legitimate, 37, 96; listening to, 53; NGOs and, 26–27, 67–68, 70, 81; nonexistent, 85–86; perpetrators and, 6, 81, 84n7, 128–29; as positive, 96–97; representation of, 37–38; testimony and, 93; time and, 88

Victims' Relatives Organization, 98

Wiesel, Elie, 43–44, 44n3

www.ingramcontent.com/pod-product-compliance
Lightning Source LLC
Chambersburg PA
CBHW051130160426
43195CB00014B/2419